Re $, explain low

CD: Biz cards... 1

☐ Campaign FaceBook page ·· Prin.

Check online → 19
Cross check w/ Grey → (21)
24
28
30
31
Office space 31 -32
Endorsement questionaire 33
(58)
(63)
Sample ballots 47

HOW TO GET ELECTED TO STATE & LOCAL OFFICE

A beginner's guide

%$ b1# FF7

Timothy R. Hickman

Catherine Hickman

Contact Katie re Kickoff

.

Timothy R. Hickman and Catherine Hickman

Visit our website at:
www.howtogetelectedtostateandlocaloffice.com

You can email us at:
info@howtogetelectedtostateandlocaloffice.com

"Many forms of Government have been tried, and will be tried in this world of sin and woe. No one pretends that democracy is perfect or all-wise. Indeed it has been said that democracy is the worst form of Government except for all those other forms that have been tried from time to time...."

Winston Churchill
(House of Commons, 11 November 1947)

CONTENTS

1 WHY DO YOU WANT TO RUN FOR OFFICE?

This book is a practical guide for the idealist. It's written for the person who believes in an inclusive democracy and wants to enfranchise as many voters as possible. It's written for the person who is committed to working so future generations will enjoy a healthy and renewable environment. It's written for the individual who wants to give their community a voice and is committed to working to improve the lives of people.

It's written for the person who believes that politics can and should be an honorable profession.

If you're considering running for a local office, ask yourself this question: "Why do I want to run and what do I hope to accomplish?"

If you want to run for office in the hope of building your business or empowering your special interest or be part of an exclusive club, you need to know that I'm not writing this book for you. It would be best if you put this book down and walk away.

This book is written to help good people who are needed in public office learn how to navigate the arduous task of running and winning their first elected office. It's a "how to" manual filled with practical advice as well as mistakes to avoid.

Half Skill Half Opportunity

First, it's important to realize that any run for an office is influenced by the situation. For instance, your opportunity to run and get elected is stronger if there is no incumbent, a very unpopular incumbent or an incumbent from the wrong party for that district. If the opportunity is right, it's possible to win even with a less than perfect campaign.

On the other hand, if there is a popular incumbent, or you're from the wrong political party for that district, it doesn't matter how skillful you are at campaigning. It will be tough to win.

Realize that running for office requires a major commitment on your behalf. If you decide to run, give it all you got. If you "sort of" run and aren't willing to give it 100%, you are wasting your time and the energy and money of your supporters.

Run a campaign that you will be proud of whether you win or lose. Run a campaign where you maintain your self-esteem and the respect of all those who supported you. If you win, know that you maintained both your honesty and integrity.

If you are on board with the vision and goals I have presented, then let's get started on how to run and win your first elected office.

2 "YOUR MILEAGE MAY VARY"

This book delves into the "why and how" to send first timers off into the world of politics in the United States. It's up to you, the reader to find out the specific rules for the office you are seeking.

America has a very diverse set of election rules and processes. Each of the 50 states is different, and there are thousands of local Election Boards and Election Authorities. As soon as you begin to consider running for office it is imperative you ascertain the up to date rules and the process of running for office from the Election Board or Election Authority that supervises or runs that election. You must know and follow the Election Laws and comply with deadlines filing any and all required campaign finance reports as well as candidate finance and conflict of interest reports that may be required.

As written, *How to Get Elected to State and Local Office* describes a standard two-step election process of a closed or open primary and then a general election to win office.

The description of how to get elected works equally for other American election processes. You will need to adjust the book's planning, scheduling and budgeting advice if you are campaigning for office in a one-step non-partisan election, or a blanket primary, jungle or top two election, (this type is crazy), or the interesting rank choice voting also known as an instant runoff election, or a process that allows for the possible third step: that of a runoff primary election.

You may also need to adjust the timing of your campaign as it is written here, with consideration of the quantity of early voting and mail-in/absentee voting that occurs in your state.

This book describes running for an election that pays a salary and requires working full time or almost full time in public office. If you are seeking a party or public office that is part-time and pays little or no salary, then the effort described in this book can be scaled down to suit the campaign for that office.

So there you have it. Follow the rules of your locale, read on to find out how to get elected and remember as you read: "your mileage may vary."

3 GETTING KNOWN, COMMUNITY LEADERSHIP

Community Leadership

There are two different techniques in becoming known within a community that can then help facilitate getting elected to the State Legislature or a local office in city or county government. The first method is to work hard for other candidates in hope to come up through the ranks. The other is to rise through your hard work becoming known in your community. It's possible to do both depending on the political landscape. In my experience, I wasn't part of the political organization, so I had to work very hard on my own within the community to become known as a viable candidate. Whatever method you choose, it's essential that you recognize the importance of becoming known within your community.

Campaign Volunteer

First, as a loyal supporter of a candidate for higher office, you campaign for that candidate and work tirelessly to be recognized not only by the candidate but also by others in the organization.

For instance, say you have chosen to support and work for a mayoral candidate. You work on the candidate's behalf at fundraising, door-to-door campaigning, phone banks, campaign events-- everything that helps the candidate while elevating your profile along the way. Then when a position is open on the Central Committee or the Mosquito Control Board or a similar local government position, you throw your hat into the ring.

At this point, you may ask to join the "ticket," or perhaps you're invited to join the team. The Mayor or the County Executive remember how hard you worked in the campaign office, walking door-to-door or at events and the organization behind the mayor is also familiar with you. The result of your hard work is to be selected to run for the Central Committee with your name appearing at the bottom of a ticket that includes the top, the Mayor. Such notoriety will also help you in future runs for the lower house of the legislature in your state or a city or town council seat.

On the other hand, if your hard work for a candidate running for a higher office does *not* result in becoming part of a ticket, you still have gained invaluable experience. Undoubtedly you have learned the politics of your community and gained insight both good and bad regarding the running of a campaign which will help you as you break out on your own.

This seemingly "fast track" also has risks. One is that you are competing with others that are likely to be working towards a similar goal—an entrée into the political arena. Secondly, if your candidate loses a race, their political collateral is gone. On the plus side, you will have the opportunity to inherit some of their organization. Finally, if for any reason your candidate turns out to be unscrupulous in any way, whether financially or personally, that can cast a shadow on *your* candidacy for political office in the future.

Community Leader

Secondly, as a community leader, you can run independently of other candidates or a political organization. If you are known within your community as a community activist, then it's a natural progression to make a run for a local elected office.

How do you become a leader in your community? Become an active member of community organizations. Make your community better by working on issues that matter to residents. The local Recreation & Parks Council is a great way to connect with parents who have their children involved in sports and extracurricular activities. Join your community or homeowner's association, local chapters of a veteran's group or political organization. Becoming an active member of your community connects you with voters through "hot issues" concerning the community and also allows you the opportunity to connect through events such as neighborhood cleanups, caroling at Christmas, 4th of July parades, etc. A school PTA, particularly if you can become elected to the PTA Council, provides a forum to become known to a large group of people coming together within the community.

I found that working-class neighborhoods in my district had strong political clubs, PTA's, volunteer fire departments and several veteran organizations. Before running for office, I joined as many organizations as I could and once I ran for office, I made presentations and met with all community organizations to hear their concerns and offer my platform. I also found that upper-middle-class neighborhoods did not have volunteer fire departments or as many veteran groups but had strong neighborhood associations, PTA's and Recreation Councils.

When I started with the Rec Council, I was one of many volunteers. During my time volunteering with Recreation and Parks, I worked with others in the organization to turn an old railroad line into a bicycle trail. Having served in many capacities, I was asked to serve as Vice President then President of the Recreation & Parks Council for the community. The leaders of 50 recreation programs met with me every month. When I ran for office, some of these same people volunteered for me. In addition, they opened doors for me to speak to other organizations where they were members.

When I first ran for office, there were five Democratic Clubs. Some clubs were stronger than others. Certain clubs were guaranteed to support the incumbent. However, there's value in becoming an active member and attending all the club meetings. First, it's the best way to be able to make a presentation to sway points of view. Secondly, always remember that *things change.* By being respectful of the opposing point of view, you are more likely to have the forum and the attention and opportunity to change people's minds. Eventually, a club I belonged to who were staunch supporters of my opponent became my supporters.

Before my first run for office, I became active in fighting against a proposal in support of a highway that would run through the community between areas of a state park and undeveloped land. If the land were developed, it would double the size of the community, overloading the infrastructure, including schools and services. There were viable concerns that local businesses would become destroyed as the highway would attract big box stores making it easy to circumvent the independently owned stores in the community.

As one of four leaders involved in leading this issue, the "Stop the Highway Committee" worked tirelessly to bring awareness to the community. We made numerous presentations to community and homeowner associations and other public meetings. We worked with community groups to sign petitions. We wrote articles and editorials supporting blockage of the highway proposal to local newspapers. The committee was eventually successful in blocking the highway. After I was elected, I successfully extended the parkland into the area originally reserved for the proposed highway.

In addition to the opportunity to become involved in a good cause, it provided great exposure and involvement with the community. Of the four leaders involved in the cause, two members successfully sought local office. One ran for the County Council, and I ran for the Maryland House of Delegates.

Additional Mitigating Factors:

Also, consider who you are and your relevance and history in the community. For instance, I was born and attended school in one part of the legislative district, yet was a homeowner, married and raising a family in another area of the legislative district. To ensure my commitment to both communities, all political literature, newspaper articles, etc. would state the community where I resided as well as the community where I was born.

Everything that connects with voters is important. Community Leadership is your first test if you're seeking local office. By the time I was seeking local office and speaking in front of neighborhood associations or clubs of any kind, my introduction would be something like this: "Catonsville resident, born in Arbutus, he's a former Recreation and Parks Council President, former President of the Democratic Club, former chair of 'Stop the Highway' committee....."

4 WHAT MAKES PEOPLE VOTE FOR YOU

There is no *one* reason to make people want to vote for you. As a candidate, it's your job to know that you need multiple exposures through a variety of channels to solidify your vote. Don't be fooled into thinking that getting in front of a voter once seals the deal. You need to be *everywhere* with your message.

Also, as a candidate, you need to recognize that the criteria voters use to vote for candidates are different depending on the office. Voting for President, for example, is not the same as voting for a member of the lower house of the State Legislature, The Town Council, or the Mosquito Control Board. You need to differentiate the importance of the seat you are running for and how it impacts the voters. That will guide you in how and where you need to be to win the vote. After you identify how and where you'll also come to realize the more voters see you, the more they see your name, the more you maximize your exposure among voters, the greater the possibility of winning their vote.

Maximize Your Exposure

Don't make the mistake of thinking that one type of media is all you need for a particular demographic. The goal is to maintain maximum exposure to voters using a variety of vehicles. The *perception* is that your message to voters is *everywhere.*

Yard signs in the neighborhood, direct mail, speaking to groups, a tea or coffee event held at a home of a neighbor, door-to-door canvassing, articles and interviews in community newspapers, an informative website and Facebook page are all important methods to maximize exposure. People also vote for candidates because they graduated from the same high school, attended the same college or live in the same community.

Voters may also vote for you because you're a member of their church or because you share a point of view on a particular issue that concerns the community. Cover as many bases as possible to ensure that voters share an affinity with you, the candidate.

If your district covers a variety of communities, you need to appeal and have an identity to all those communities. Also, if it makes sense for the district you are running in, and other candidates are popular in that district for other offices, consider becoming part of a ticket or team of candidates running for office. A ticket can be a winning proposition particularly if a candidate on the ticket is wildly popular where you are not and you, on the other hand, can "carry" them by offering another community where you are well known, and they are not.

Don't think this allows you to ignore or take for granted these voters. Running on a ticket provides an entrée to campaign in that community.

Circumstances Out of Your Control

Some circumstances are simply out of your control as a candidate. Some circumstances will help your campaign, while others may hinder it. A good candidate manipulates circumstances to maximize advantage and minimize the negatives.

For instance, running in a district with no incumbent is the best circumstance. Second is running in a district where the incumbent is unpopular. You will still be competing against a known entity but the unpopularity of the incumbent is to your advantage, and you can use that effectively as you campaign.

Finally, if the incumbent is popular, you will have the difficult task of winning over voters to choose you. It will be an uphill battle to position you as the worthy alternative choice. In this scenario, it's best not to directly "go after" your opponent but rather find issues the community can connect to and present yourself as the candidate who will provide the solutions to those issues.

One of the best things that happened to me during my campaign when I was running for The House of Delegates was being attacked by the incumbent State Senator. It singled me out from some of the candidates running for that office as the main alternative for voters who either didn't want to vote for him or someone else

10

on his ticket. After I was elected, he shared with me his regret in attacking me. It did in fact, propel my campaign. Undoubtedly, however, it was the hard work that followed that attack that won the election.

Circumstances in Your Control

I know legislators who had the best possible situation and worked very little to win an election. I also know candidates who worked very hard and lost elections. While the circumstances around your election play a key factor in your chance to win, never underestimate the power of hard work and working smart. My mantra which I conveyed to everyone in the campaign office was that if they couldn't justify the next minute of activity or the next dollar spent on winning a vote then don't do the activity or spend the dollar. _Every_ action or dollar spent must be directly related to gaining votes.

Candidates at times make the mistake of thinking their campaign is a tool to educate voters on issues. A campaign is not the time to educate voters. I have seen opposing candidates spend significant sums of money for newspaper ads "educating" voters yet do little else in the way of meeting voters or door knocking. I have also seen candidates in a door to door canvass spend twenty minutes or a half an hour with one voter. In the meantime, they missed the opportunity to knock on many more doors.

Campaigns are fueled by effectively using the tools at hand to gain the trust of voters. It's about using all the contacts you have and maximizing the money you have accumulated to fund the campaign. It's about effectively using your army of volunteers working in the campaign. Your contacts, the budget, your volunteers all must work to get your name out to as many people as possible and win votes.

Exposure, Exposure, Exposure

Candidates who are running for office sometime stand with some of their volunteers on street corners with signs and wave. While this may be one way of getting your name out, I believe it to be pedestrian.

Personal contact is the key. Shake hands, talk to the neighborhood association, door knock, and send direct mail. Seek out endorsements in the neighborhood via yard signs, or bumper stickers. Place ads in the local paper, show up at community functions and parades, work to get yourself known within your community and encourage your committed voters to spread the word as to who has won their vote.

It's vital to do everything possible to have contact with voters. Stand outside your local grocery store and meet and greet voters and hand out campaign literature. Be respectful of the voter's time and the fact that you can't be sure of party affiliation or their stand on issues. Introduce yourself, the office you're seeking, perhaps a sentence on why you're running and offer a brochure.

There was a large defense contractor near my community, and 20% of their workforce resided in my district. I checked with their public relations office and was allowed to be at the gate on specific dates when people arrived for work and when they left in the evenings. I went with six to eight volunteers. Their job was to stand in front and ask people if they lived in one of the communities in my district and when they found someone they would ask if they would like to meet the candidate, Tim Hickman, (or later on Delegate or Senator Tim Hickman). They also handed out brochures where it made sense. Having my volunteers do the prescreening was helpful in allowing me to shake as many hands as possible from my district. It was fun, upbeat and provided an opportunity to "press the flesh" of voters in my district.

Some voters know who they will choose for governor, but don't know who they are voting for further down on the ballot until the last minute. They are in the voting booth; they'll see your name and then remember yard signs or your bumper stickers on cars and have an affinity to your name. Or they may think, "My neighbors are voting for him, so I will too."

How much the success of your campaign is based on name recognition and how much is because you're on the right side of the issues will be difficult to determine. However, remember it's about being in front of the voters in many different ways. You also need to be on the right side of the issues and work smart and work hard. Whether it's a conscious decision or an unconscious one on behalf of voters casting ballots –you'll win more votes.

5 TICKET NO TICKET

A s a candidate, you must weigh the pros and cons of whether to run as part of a ticket, also known as a slate, or go it alone. First, have you been invited to join a slate or is there an opportunity that you can seek? Should you try to form your own ticket or is it better to go it alone? These are issues that are best considered early in the campaign. There are clear advantages as well as disadvantages to joining a slate.

Advantages

The first advantage to running as part of a ticket is the ability to rely on your teammates to help you secure votes in neighborhoods where they are more known than you and vice versa. The district I ran in consisted of five distinct neighborhoods. While I had ties to community service clubs, PTA's, Recreation Councils and churches, I lacked strong ties to some of the other communities. Printed on my brochures, was "born in Arbutus and lives in Catonsville." That said there were still three neighborhoods where I had less of a connection. In fact, most of us on the team were from the largest two communities in the district. However, members of the ticket who ran for the Democratic State Central Committee had ties with the other neighborhoods.

Running as part of a ticket or slate has other benefits too. As part of a ticket your resources are pooled so there is less money individually needed through fundraising to run an effective campaign. However, since the Central Committee is a non-paying office, those candidates were not required to contribute funds. They campaigned for the team, and their efforts were invaluable in connecting us to the voters in the neighborhoods where we were not as well connected.

There will also be a collaborative effort on running the campaign, therefore, saving time in strategizing. In this team approach, you'll require less of an individual army of volunteers too.

When candidates run as a part of a ticket, all responsibilities and expenditures are agreed upon collectively. The candidates determine the total amount of money needed for running the campaign. The budget must include the necessary funds for the printing of literature, media buys and the like, and then the total is divided among the candidates as to how much each candidate must raise. In this scenario, there is a Treasurer for the slate who files finance reports for the slate, and each candidate pays their share into the campaign and files reports individually as well.

In addition to requiring fewer volunteers, when you're part of a ticket you have the opportunity to share in the pool of talent that each candidate brings to the table. Perhaps a candidate or a close supporter can provide graphic design assistance, or media advice, or design a website for the team.

How tight the team is as an organization will decide if bumper stickers are printed as a group or for individual candidates. Likewise for campaign buttons: we decided to have both individual buttons and team buttons printed.

Additionally, there were times we ran candidates for State Central Committee not for their neighborhood contacts but because they were effective, dedicated campaign workers. The Central Committee provides an entrée into public office and a stepping stone into paid political office.

Disadvantages

The most obvious risk is the possibility to be tied to a candidate at the top of the ticket that is unpopular. Whether the candidate is unpopular at the start or becomes unpopular as he campaigns, if you're running on the ticket, you have tied your fate to that candidate.

A particular problem, if you're in a multi-member district on a ticket, can occur when you are not the only candidate on the ticket vying for a seat. For example, you are one of three candidates running for a seat in the lower house of the State Legislature in the primary election. While your ticket includes three candidates running for three seats the opposition has a ticket which includes two incumbents and one new candidate. Though it's possible one or both of the incumbents won't be re-elected, it's more likely they will be re-elected. In essence, you are *competing with your ticket mates* as well as the other candidates on the opposition's ticket. The same scenario can occur in a multi-member district in a general election.

You campaign as part of the team, handing out literature in the door-to-door canvass, etc. Can you rely on the other candidates running for the lower house on the ticket to mention your name? It's also possible that another member of your ticket will favor the other new candidate and campaign more on his behalf. And, if you, in fact, worked to campaign on behalf of the entire ticket fairly, you have provided them access to your friends, supporters, organizations and neighborhoods in your district. Your honest efforts as part of a ticket may result in pushing the other candidate over the top to win the open seat.

Even worse, the other candidate on your ticket competing with you for the open seat may single shoot. That is the process in which the candidate instructs family, friends and supporters to vote *only* for them even though the ballot instructions are to "vote for no more than three." Single shooting creates a path for winning by inflating one's votes by limiting the number of votes overall in a multi-member district ballot.

Single shooting is a major issue when the election is for a public office with multi-member districts. It takes a leap of faith as the candidate competing for an open seat, and you must be vigilant as well to be sure you are giving and receiving support from other members of the team.

Additionally, the candidate at the top of the ticket has the responsibility to keep everyone working as a team. He or she must try to reinforce "we're all in this together." When I was at the top of the ticket, our team campaigned hard, and we remained optimistic that we could win all three seats.

The Hybrid Ticket

There are also situations where you can run on a hybrid ticket of sorts. For instance, you can give more support to a candidate running for a countywide office than that candidate can give you running in a district. However, in addition to its being the right thing to do, you may pick up voters who are friends, family and supporters of the candidate running for a countywide seat. In this scenario, you may support each other yet print separate campaign literature but offer each other's literature as you campaign.

My Experiences: Ticket No Ticket

The first time I ran for office I was a college student. I had a large, enthusiastic group of students and adults in the community supporting my campaign. I ran independently for one of three seats in the lower house of the State Legislature. I worked hard, but I didn't always work smart. I found too many excuses not to campaign door-to-door. Seventeen candidates were running for three seats, and I came in seventh.

The next time I ran on a short ticket with a candidate running for the County Council. We also ran with two candidates running for the Central Committee. My goal here was to align myself with candidates who may help me with their voters, and I help them as well.

My earlier election loss also helped me realize the necessity of campaigning and giving it my total effort. I became fanatical with campaigning door-to-door, seven days a week for months, rain or shine, no exception. I was not in the campaign office if it was possible to be out earning votes. I won the seat in the lower house of the State Legislature knocking off an establishment candidate who was part of an opposing ticket. The candidate who ran for County Council as part of the ticket also won. And while the two candidates for the Central Committee did not win, one of them returned four years later and won a seat on the County Council. The other became my legislative aide.

My next election was with a complete slate. I was the candidate for State Senate. One candidate ran for County Council, three candidates for the House of Delegates and five candidates ran for the Central Committee. We won a large percentage of offices that year.

Whether to run a ticket or not has many variables that you the candidate must contemplate. Circumstances surrounding the office you are seeking at the time are paramount in your consideration. It's best to decide early so that you can strategize based on your decision.

6 POLITICAL CAMPAIGN MANAGEMENT SOFTWARE

I n preparation for campaigning it's important to explore the software packages available that can assist you with accessing voter information. There are dozens of political campaign management software packages available. They are designed to ease, improve and expand a variety of campaign tasks. As such technology continues to evolve and improve, you must research and decide what current software (if any) suits your campaign's needs.

For example, the Democratic National Committee (DNC) has decided on a top-down unified software offering for all levels of democratic campaigns. Called VAN and also known as VoteBuilder, it is offered through all State Democratic Parties throughout the U.S. The company that develops this software for the Democratic Party, NGP-VAN, also offers additional campaign management software.

If you are running as an independent, or in a non-partisan election, you'll need to research political campaign software. If you are running as a Republican, then call your state party headquarters for their recommendations.

With the DNC choosing the software, if you're a Democrat preparing to campaign, contact your state's Democratic Party headquarters and inquire with the Data Coordinator, Data Director, Voter File Manager, etc., regarding how to learn about and purchase VoteBuilder/VAN. This browser-based software provides Democrats access to a complete profile of registered voters in the district from party affiliation, to voting history, to preferences, to ethnicity to the number of voters in the household as well as a volunteer management tool.

Using any computer and internet browser, you can create both walk lists for the door-to-door canvass and call lists.

VAN software also allows you to virtually draw your canvassing map and create edits as necessary based on your knowledge of an area. Additionally, there is a mobile canvassing app called MiniVAN allowing you to go door-to-door using a smartphone or tablet and eliminating the need for paper folders and maps and the task to physically record ranking the voters.

While the software is available throughout the country, each State's Board of Elections or Election Authority decides on *what* information from the states voter registration list is accessible. For instance, a state may not allow certain information to be included such as party affiliation, voting history, or date of birth, etc.; therefore what voter information the software can provide varies.

Software such as VoteBuilder/VAN offers many ways to stay connected to the registered voters in the Democratic Party. What happens in a closed primary if your state will not provide party registration? *Campaign software can project likely party affiliation onto the lists by analyzing preferences as tracked through data mining methods.*

Finally, the cost of the software varies from the state party to state party. The fee charged can be a flat fee or priced by the number of voters in a district.

Other political campaign software such as provided by NGP/VAN can also allow for the management of contributors. Using this software, you can also automate your campaign's budget, accounting and the filing of the legally required campaign finance reports.

This additional software also allows you to plan and implement your campaign's social networking through its Social Organizing Tools. You can also build a website, accept contributions online and email supporters through a supporter engagement platform.

However, if you are a candidate with a small local office or you are running for a non-paying office, it may be more cost effective to call your local Board of Elections or Election Authority and purchase an electronic or paper Voters List directly. In addition to being too costly, Political Campaign Management Software may provide more information and options than you deem necessary for your campaign.

7 RAISING MONEY

The most uncomfortable task for many candidates running for a local office is raising money. However, before you begin the arduous task of raising money, it is imperative to learn the rules of your local jurisdiction and the Election Authority regarding the raising of funds for a campaign and filing disclosure deadlines.

For instance, in most states, a candidate wishing to run for office must have either a Campaign Treasurer or a Committee with a Chairman and a Treasurer. Consult your State Election Office, such as The State Election Board or the Secretary of State's Office or your County or Local Election Authority. They will most likely present you with a booklet of instructions for the legal requirements including filing disclosures of campaign contributions. These rules vary from state to state and are constantly changing through legislation. It's very important to be working with the latest and correct set of rules.

The Organization Behind the Money

Whether it's the candidate who selects a Treasurer or the Campaign Committee, it's imperative that the person chosen is responsible and trustworthy. The Treasurer must be detail oriented, keep the books in good order and is in charge of maintaining all the filing deadlines as provided by the Local Election Authority. Opposing candidates and the media enjoy reporting when a candidate has missed a filing deadline or in the event of a mistake in the accounting resulting in a financial penalty. The internet allows easy access to information regarding filing deadlines or accounting errors. Unfortunately, even when an "honest" mistake occurs, a candidate's reputation will suffer as a result of such a negative story.

Some candidates appoint their spouse as Treasurer. While convenient, it's of the utmost importance that there is no public relations issue for the spouse. The duties of Treasurer must be performed efficiently and be beyond reproach. As a candidate, you will not have the time to look over the books or double check deadlines. Appoint a Treasurer that you trust completely. If at any time in the campaign the Treasurer fails to perform their duties, it's imperative he or she be replaced immediately. Failure to do so can compromise the reputation of the candidate.

The financial issues relate directly to the integrity of you as a candidate and your campaign. Campaign software such as NGP/VAN's Campaign Financial Software package manages the list of financial contributors as well as assists in preparing the legally required financial reports. Such software may be helpful to your Campaign Treasurer, but you will need to trust him, or her so choose wisely.

Another important reason to file as a candidate and appoint a Treasurer is that you can't begin to raise money until you file as a candidate. In some cases, candidates will postpone filing because of a job-related reason or because the candidate is hoping to run as part of a group on a ticket. Both are valid reasons to delay filing, but it's important to achieve the balance between announcing, filing and appointing a Treasurer so that valuable fundraising can begin.

There is also a strategy for filing early campaign reports. For example, you are in a race challenging an incumbent along with two other candidates. You have raised a generous amount of campaign contributions, far more than the other candidates and rivaling the amount in the campaign fund of the incumbent. The media will report on the amount raised in your campaign to date. It provides credentials and respectability that you are in fact a serious contender. This same scenario of your candidacy and campaign funds to date can intimidate your opponents or individuals toying with the idea to run.

In some states, it is permissible to set up a Exploratory committee and begin fundraising without officially filing as a candidate. In fact, this gives the potential candidate an opportunity to test the waters. Another reason to begin this way is that there are doors that close once you officially declare candidacy. Media, for instance, will treat you differently as a candidate as they will work to appear impartial. There are also opportunities to speak that will not readily be available once you are a declared candidate.

Finally, when you set up the Campaign Committee, find out if there is a distinction between a Campaign Committee and an Ongoing Campaign Committee. States will have different laws. In the State of Maryland, for instance, an Ongoing Committee allows the candidate the opportunity to donate excess funds after the election to another candidate running for office or the ability to keep excess funds for future runs for office.

Creating the Budget

The first step in creating a budget is researching the costs associated with running an effective campaign. Following are a list of media and operating costs. Brainstorm what you think you will need, research and finally evaluate the costs.

Operating Costs:
- Campaign Office
- Paid Office Manager
- Campaign Manager, Fundraising Consultant (optional paid positions)
- Desks and chairs (work to obtain donated furniture or second hand)
- Phone line (prepaid phone for office use or add an additional cell phone to your cell phone package)
- Computers and internet (work to obtain donated computers)
- Miscellaneous office supplies
- Voter Lists (whether purchasing an electronic list or a Campaign Software Package which includes the voters list and additional features)

Media Expenses
- Design and printing of campaign brochures
- Direct Mail costs, (price out printers, type of mailing such as postcard, trifold, letter, etc. and postage fees for a Standard /Bulk Rate Permit vs. the costs associated with employing a mail house to handle design, printing, and mailing)
- Cost of bumper stickers, and yard signs
- Domain name and website
- Print ads in local newspapers and magazines
- Radio and TV spots
- Local billboards
- Social Media Advertising including Facebook ads and other targeted online advertising
- Cost associated with fundraisers

Operating Costs:

While it is advisable to work as much as possible with the goal of having a volunteer staff, there are a couple of exceptions to consider. Much of your time as the candidate is devoted to campaigning and spending time among the voters. There is much to be done to organize as well as make effective use of the time offered by your volunteers. You need a person who is willing to spend the better part of every day at the office. If not one person then perhaps 2 or 3 people share in the responsibility. If you can find a mature person, who is interested in the job and doesn't need to get paid that's great. However, most people will be more dedicated, and responsible if they are receiving a small salary.

In one campaign there was a college student who was very interested in gaining experience, and for a stipend, it worked well for her to work and manage the office and be paid a small amount in return. In another campaign, I had the good fortune of having a college professor's wife who was a professional writer and recovering from an illness work in the office every day. She loved working with my young volunteers and was a den mother of sorts. Her organizational skills were unmatched, and she was able to organize the volunteers to help in a myriad of ways. Some candidates had their spouses pitch in and manage the office when necessary.

In short, it depends on circumstances and availability. But you may want to provide a line in your budget early on in the event you need to pay a modest salary for an Office Manager.

Campaign Managers and Consultants are also paid positions, but most often they are too expensive for local races. Campaign Managers are strategists. Candidates seeking local offices often provide their own strategy but rely on competent people (like an Office Manager) to run the day to day operations and supervise volunteers.

Whenever possible, take advantage of the talent pool offered by your family, friends, and supporters. However, if you lack the skills or the talent pool for certain campaign tasks you may need to consider hiring consultants. This is only for consideration if your budget allows and if you're running for a paying office in a sizable district. When creating the budget, every effort must be made to maximize dollars spent and the more you hire outside experts the faster you blow through the budget. That said, the positions you may want to consider hiring professionals are: Graphic Designer, Campaign Manager, Fundraising Consultant, and Mail House Services.

Media Expenses

Keep in mind that all the media suggested here may not be suited for the local office you are seeking. For example, pay attention to how large or small the readership may be or the area covered by a newspaper. It's unwise to pay for a newspaper ad for instance if in fact the coverage far exceeds your district boundaries. I did not have the luxury to effectively use TV for commercials. The metropolitan area for TV included too many voters that weren't in my district. However, a colleague of mine on the eastern shore was able to utilize the singular local station effectively for his campaign.

Also, be sure to consider *the quantities* of mailings, ads, etc. that you may need during the campaign. Considering how much or how little you need to successfully market your campaign is dependent on whether you are an incumbent or a challenger. Is the election decided upon with the primary or is the general election likely to also be a contest? In my case, residing in a very Democratic state, most elections here are decided in the primary.

Finally, and most importantly, consider how you may be able to reduce these costs through contributions. For instance, a volunteer who owns a printing company may offer you printing at cost, or a caterer who allows you to use their facility for a reduced price offsets the cost associated with a dinner or cocktail fundraiser. Be conscious that a reduction of cost may be regarded as an "in-kind" donation. Your Treasurer must report it in accordance with your local Election Authorities' requirements. On the other hand, donations are no different than a person writing a check and as such must be reported as a campaign contribution.

One of the most important reasons to develop a budget is that as the candidate it's important to know what you need before you need it. There is so much energy and work in campaigning that any money raised beforehand allows you to concentrate on the task of connecting with the voters. And you can't raise money until you have an idea of what you need.

Where to Begin Raising Funds & Pitfalls to Avoid

Do you hit up your relatives, friends, colleagues, and anyone you have ever met for a contribution? Yes. Do you have the ability to fund yourself? Do you have a parent, brother in law or someone close with deep pockets that can help fund your campaign? If so, this can help jumpstart your campaign. Be aware, however, that contributions must be reported periodically to the Election Authority as public information and as such will be disclosed by newspapers and other media as well as your opposing candidate.

As a candidate, you'll find that businesses will want to contribute to your campaign. The bigger the business, the bigger the pocketbook and more eager they are to contribute to your campaign. Tread very carefully here as businesses are often hoping to trade access to you with campaign contributions. That's the best case scenario. Worst case is they are hoping to trade their contributions for your vote in matters that can affect their business. Do you sell out? I strongly recommend against it.

Whenever this occurs in politics, it forces the candidate to become beholden to a business, or special interest group. The public will see it for what it is: a conflict of interest where you appear to be trading votes for money. Campaign contribution reports are public.

On the other hand, be sure your Campaign Committee looks into who the contributors are in your opponent's campaign. If in fact, they are taking contributions from a large business in town or a special interest group, be ready to pounce on that fact and get it in front of voters.

When I ran for office, my approach was to solicit many small contributions from individuals. While it makes for more work, at the end of the day I was not beholden to any special interest group or big business. Make certain that contributors to your campaign know that they are not buying your support. They need to believe in where you stand on the issues but realize that their support will not buy your vote once in office.

I worked very hard to gain voter trust and enjoyed constituent support and union support. As a bonus for working so hard to gain individual contributions, the many constituents who donated to my campaign were "vested" and committed to our success and as such I knew I could count on their votes.

When Do You Start Fundraising?

While it is difficult to hold events before you declare there are ways to raise money and test the waters for support. For instance, you can have a committee exploring the possibility of a run for office. If you have actively been working to build your reputation in the community (see Chapter: *Getting Known, Community Leadership*), then perhaps there is a dinner held in your honor as a thank you for your outstanding service with the Rec Council, or your efforts in another community issue. As mentioned earlier, I was one of the leaders in the "Stop the Highway" efforts in my community. At the time, it was a volatile issue and became a source of notoriety along with my Recreation Council leadership. In addition to speeches and kudos, the room is filled with people who are in appreciation of your efforts. There is no better launching pad for running for an elected office.

Once you have declared, jumpstart raising campaign funds by hosting an event early before the door-to-door campaigning begins in earnest. Consider an indoor or outdoor event that can attract many with a nominal fee such as a family picnic at a park or local farm. One example is a family fun day with arcade style games, pony rides, and face painting. The goal here is twofold: to raise funds and bring a greater awareness to you, the candidate. If done well it will also help you in raising the volunteer army you will need for the campaign.

Events held early in the campaign cycle, need to serve as an introduction to you, help build the army of volunteers and supporters and serve as the base for future events. For example, let's say you host a Family Fun Day at the community park in your town. Your brother in law underwrites the event. The connections you make that day result in 5 people agreeing to host coffees not to mention the people who may volunteer or buy tickets to a bull roast or cocktail party. Results such as these make an event held early in the campaign valuable in many ways.

How Many Events Will You Need?

Start with the budget you and your committee created. Break down the costs monthly for running the campaign. Then start brainstorming the number of events, the amount of money needed from the events, as well as the goals necessary for private contributions. All these factors will be helpful in achieving your goal of fundraising whether you need $20,000 or $100,000 in the coffers.

Always remember that the private contributions you receive early will also serve as the basis for voters you can count on and will also be a fine resource for your volunteer army. Another advantage to appearing to be well funded by many supporters is that it can work to discourage possible opponents from entering the race.

How to Sell Out Political Fundraisers

As the campaign is in full swing and you're committee is actively working on events, keep in mind that attendance and *perception* of great attendance are both of equal importance. Also when an event is sold out, besides adding money to the campaign to be used in direct mail, yard signs or the like, you have the opportunity to solidify votes. People love to support a winner. Well attended events are contagious for getting the word out.

One method I used for selling out events was to give each member of my committee an equal amount of tickets to sell. If each member of a ten-member committee sells 20 tickets, the event can reach a goal of 200. It's important to encourage those selling tickets to do whatever they need to sell their tickets. They can bring their mother; sell to a neighbor, co-worker, sister or brother. Again, a fundraiser is meant to raise money, create awareness of the candidate and the issues to the voters. And it's essential that events are sellouts!

If the committee is not having success selling out the event, consider either selling lower priced or even complimentary tickets to office holders, organization heads, the party's Central Committee, or the Town Council. Officeholders, in particular, do not expect to pay for tickets so consider who can help your run for office. It's helpful to have the support of officeholders or the *perception* of their support. This "support," adds validity to your campaign.

Is time running out to sell tickets and you still have a few tables to fill? Consider "rewarding" volunteers with a complimentary ticket. It's imperative that your committee works to make the event successful. A sold-out event brings in revenue, excites your base, confirms votes and will also bring more people in as those who attended the event share the experience with their family and friends.

Another consideration is working with groups in the hope of an endorsement and inviting them to an event. I ran in a suburban district which included blue-collar and upper-middle-class voters. Teacher associations, unions, and environmental groups ultimately endorsed my run for office. These groups were supporters who bought tickets and attended my events.

It can be a challenge early on if you are a new candidate to be endorsed or supported by certain associations or groups. But say, for example, you have a friend who is a teacher and he or she is willing to sell 30 tickets to their friends or colleagues. The *perception* is that you are gaining their support although the teacher's union hasn't yet committed to you.

Stretching Dollars for Campaign Fundraisers

Rent the town hall, the Moose Hall or the National Guard Armory for a cocktail party. Ask a few supporters to make hors-d'oeuvres. Find out if there is someone with a relationship with a liquor store owner or someone comfortable with asking an owner if they are willing to work with you to allow you to take a variety of alcohol on consignment. The arrangement is that if a seal is broken, you pay for the bottle; if the seal is intact the store takes it back, and you are refunded.

I had college student volunteers work the cocktail party. They carried trays of appetizers with napkins. Wearing "uniforms" of matching trousers and shirts with white aprons, they added a touch of elegance to the Moose Lodge.

Outside the event, college-age students greeted drivers and directed people where to park. More importantly, they asked everyone who pulled in if they could put a bumper sticker on their car.

While it's helpful to have local businesses and unions contribute to your campaign, it's imperative to have the event sold out. I once had the owner of the local hair studio where I went for haircuts offer to write a personal check to support our campaign and buy a table at our bull roast fundraiser. I thanked him but expressed how important it was to fill the table as well. He closed the studio early and gave the tickets to his stylists. Heads turned at the bull roast when the owner and ten attractive coiffured hair stylists walked in.

I had a similar situation when a local union wanted to buy a block of tickets. I strongly encouraged them to give the tickets to people who would attend. Monetary support is important but never as important as having people stand with you on issues that make a difference in their community.

Additional Thoughts on Fundraisers

If you have a cocktail party or event where there is a big name speaker, consider a two-tiered fundraiser. A ticket provides admission to the event, and a VIP ticket provides a private audience with the speaker either before or after the event.

I also implemented a $10 a month club for supporters who were willing to contribute but who might have difficulty contributing larger sums of money. As the candidate, you must take an active role in fundraising both for ongoing contributions as well as sell tickets to events. You need to lead your volunteers by example.

Create a comprehensive list of everyone you can think of that will support your ideas for good government. Relatives, colleagues past and present, friends, neighbors, people you attended school with are all possibilities for financial support. I made lists, and part of *every day* was devoted to calling these people for contributions.

I found it very uncomfortable at times but also knew how important it was to the viability of the campaign. I called asking for contributions, or with the goal of selling tickets and often asked if they were willing to sell a block of tickets to their family or friends. Prepare yourself also for the necessity to call people who contribute more than once.

Always begin the conversation by thanking them for their past support, then offer an upbeat message on how the campaign is doing and the shared vision you have with them for the future. I found phone calling my contacts asking for contributions to be the most difficult job of campaigning. However, it was heartening at times to reconnect with people from my past and gain their support.

In addition to fundraising, you can also help fund your campaign with your own money. However, the laws vary from state to state so be sure to check with your State or Local Election Authority for the latest laws and regulations. Another consideration, (again after checking election laws), is the possibility of loaning your campaign money. For instance, you're in the home stretch of the campaign, and it's apparent that another $10,000 is necessary. Depending on the Election Laws in your state, you can loan your campaign the money, and after the election, you can continue to have events and pay yourself back.

You as the candidate along with your campaign committee have a fiduciary responsibility to settle all debts related to your campaign. It's also possible, again based on your state or local election laws to have fundraisers even after an election is lost to retire campaign debt. In conclusion, create a reasonable budget, spend responsibly and trust the people on your committee to keep an eye on the bottom line.

8 THE CAMPAIGN IN LONG VIEW: DEVELOP A PLAN

As written previously, an important factor in running for office is the groundwork you lay before announcing your candidacy. It's your community involvement and the network of relationships you have acquired and nurtured. I was active in the Rec Council and started a political club to raise awareness of the issues facing the community and worked to position myself as the leader on behalf of the community. The preparation ahead of time is essential to effectively running a campaign and winning an election.

One or Two Years Before the Campaign

The Campaign Committee: Forming the actual campaign committee is best done one or two years before filing as a candidate. When it's time to name the committee, be sure it's positive. My committee was "Citizens for Responsible Leadership." In most States, you will have to print the authority line on direct mail pieces and the like, so it's imperative it's a positive affirmation. The "Committee for Good Government," or the "Committee for Responsible Leadership," are two examples of affirmations which are indirectly suggesting that there are problems with the current leadership without attacking the present officeholders.

Just as forming the campaign committee is done far before the announcement of candidacy so is the process of beginning to raise funds. It's so important to begin this process while "testing" the waters to run because the campaign will need an inordinate amount of money to fuel it. It's virtually impossible to fund a campaign sufficiently if you don't have money at the beginning. There are only two exemptions to this rule that I'm familiar with: if you have an exceptional environment such as a sudden loss of the incumbent or a brand new district with no one providing competition with you among the voters.

How do you have a fundraiser before announcing your candidacy? For example, the "Committee for Good Government" has a fundraiser honoring Nancy Gilson for her contributions and tireless efforts in her work with the Rec Council. There are no bumper stickers, no campaign speeches, just the community coming together to pay tribute to Nancy Gilson and all her hard work. It's a feel good for the community, Nancy connects with the residents, (voters) in her community and the process of establishing campaign funds has begun. This is often called an "Exploratory Committee." Is it too late?

The Voters List: You must decide how to purchase the Voters List for your campaign with consideration of your budget and your need. Will you utilize campaign management software such as VoteBuilder/VAN available from your State Democratic Party (if you are running as a Democrat), for the Voters List, Walk List, Call List and Volunteer Management?

Also, investigate the value of using campaign management software such as software sold by the company NGP/VAN directly for contribution management, accepting contributions online, campaign bookkeeping, financial reporting, email engagement, social networking organization tool, and assistance with setting up a campaign website.

The other method of acquiring the Voters List is to have someone senior in the campaign purchase the Voters List from the local or State Election Authority or your party office if they provide this service. If you have contact with candidates in other districts, you can share the cost by purchasing the electronic Voters List for the entire county or city and have lists and labels printed as a group. You will need the data printed by street, first with even house numbers and then with odd house numbers. While it's important to plan where to purchase the list, and how you'll need the list prepared, don't purchase the list until you're ready to hit the streets. You want the most current list as possible.

Also, I bought monthly updates of new registrants in my district. We sent them a mailing which consisted of a new voter letter and a campaign brochure.

As part of the preparation for the campaign, you may want to estimate the number of mailings you'll do in addition to the quantity so that you can have labels printed. If there are two people in the household of the same name and same party, have the labels printed so that you can mail one piece of campaign literature, (assuming they are a couple), to "Bob and Mary Jones or the Jones Family." This will provide a considerate savings on the cost of printing and mailing. However, if there is a younger voter in the household, then send that voter a separate mailer.

Six Months to a Year Before the Campaign

When do you file to run for an elected office? Most often it will be six months to a year before the campaign. Be sure to check all the legal deadlines and rules by checking with your local Election Board, Voting Authority, or with your State's Election Board or Secretary of State. There will be forms to fill out and a fee for filing. *Did the leading Dem already file? Was this done according to the Rules?*

The exact timing that's best for you is another consideration. You don't want to file too early when people aren't yet thinking about the election. You also want to maximize your exposure with the local press. For instance, I was known in the community for the, "Stop the Highway," movement and received a fair amount of media attention. Once I declared my candidacy, the media felt inclined to give the opposition equal exposure to provide fairness in reporting to both candidates. On the other hand, if you file early it might discourage others from throwing their hat in the ring.

When you're ready to go to the Election Board or Election Authority office to file as a candidate, do it with fanfare. Have a press release ready, arrive with volunteers, have photographs taken and send the media release and photographs off to local media outlets.

Strategizing with other candidates to consider whether or not to form a ticket is best done six months to a year before the start of a campaign. At this time you will regularly meet with your committee to decide on the issues of the campaign that are most relevant and meaningful to the community.

Find a campaign office. Unless you're running a very small campaign out of your home, or a backroom of a business you'll need to rent office space for a campaign headquarters. Think about how much space you'll require and the equipment you will need to run an effective office. Unless you have generous funds, don't think luxury, think economy. Who will be occupying this space? While you need an office, you will only be there in the mornings and late evenings so again it's not necessary to have a large space. However, you will need an office to have private meetings when necessary.

Can everyone else work within a wide open space with tables in place of desks? Who else needs an office? You'll need enough space for the volunteers, a phone, computers, desks or tables, chairs, a copier and a file cabinet. You'll need a coffee maker and a small fridge for sodas. You want your volunteers to be comfortable. More importantly, you want to create energy and team spirit, so communal space is important.

If you are fortunate to find the "right" space, it's possible that you'll be able to use it for functions such as the victory party which will allow you not to have to rent a room elsewhere.

Look for a space in the district that has been empty for some time and approach the owner to see if he or she would be willing to allow you to rent the space for a specific amount of time at an economical rate. A Real Estate agent could be helpful in locating a space that has been vacant for a while. You want a storefront that offers good street availability and easy access for volunteers. It's also important that the location you choose for the office allows for a prominent sign. There are three major caveats for choosing a space for campaign headquarters: convenience, parking and a strong presence in the community.

Some of our best campaign offices had multiple rooms with space for a reception desk. A reception area provided the opportunity for the front person to direct a reporter for instance, to a private meeting room. As the candidate, I had a private office for meetings, fundraiser calls and the like. There was also a private room for the Campaign Committee and volunteer business and another room for storage of yard signs etc.

Landlords are sometimes reluctant to rent to short time tenants like political candidates but remind them there are many advantages: there will be signage bringing attention to the building, lights on in the evenings and people coming and going. These are all activities that will help bring attention to the property and attract a long-term tenant once the campaign is over and you have moved out.

Work on the content of your future brochures. If someone involved in the committee has the ability to write copy or can graphically design the brochure that will save having to hiring an outside copywriter or graphic designer. Tap the talent among the group of people that are already proving to be the core of your support. In addition to writing and designing campaign literature, you will need press releases written.

You also will need someone who can work with you to fill out endorsement interview questionnaires from organizations. Unions, for example, send out questionnaires to decide who they will back in an election. Answering these questionnaires can prove to be very helpful as an opportunity to state your positions publicly on issues and be endorsed by organizations. When I ran for office, not only were their multiple endorsement questionnaires to be completed, but I was asked to attend an AFL-CIO meeting with the heads of various unions in attendance to be interviewed. Fortunately, my stand on the issues was in line with their objectives, and I did receive backing.

However, as a candidate use caution as you seek endorsements. As stated earlier, be true to your stand on the issues. Don't pander to groups to seek their support. Endorsement questionnaires also serve as a public written record of your viewpoints. And you can be sure if there is cause to change how you vote on an issue once in office it will become known that you waffled.

Secondly, be careful which endorsements questionnaires you fill out. There are bound to be groups that you may choose not to be affiliated with at all. And be aware that certain groups will do nothing to support you and win over voters, but are merely looking to get you on the record and when you're elected hold your feet to the fire when voting on an issue they asked you about on a questionnaire.

Now is also the time to have professional photos taken of you, the candidate as well as photos to be used in brochures. Consider images of you among voters in the community at school or church functions and the like. The key is to develop as much of the future brochures and direct mail postcards and campaign literature as possible. And the same goes for development of bumper stickers and yard signs.

Finalizing campaign literature before the campaign is in full swing allows the candidate more time to meet with voters and press the flesh. Having everything ready to go, (some printed, others print ready), allows you the candidate to be ready to hit the street.

Six Months Before the Primary Election

Now is the time to start daily canvassing. I started In April and canvassed right up until the election in September. I walked door to door in my district every day, rain or shine. When I completed knocking on all the doors I needed to knock on in the district, I started the process over and did it again.

Realize that some elections are won in the primary, and some are won in the general election. In my district, the contest to be won was the primary. In fact, the opposing parties at times failed to file a candidate. Also, be aware of the time you have to campaign for the primary and the time you have to campaign for the general election.

Next question: should you knock on every door? Don't shotgun, focus. If your State has a closed primary and you have a tough competitive race ahead, don't knock on every door. Find the voters in your party and connect with them.

However, if your state has a closed primary and you're heavily favored to win your party's primary, but expect a tough race in the general election, knock on every door where there is a registered voter. The primary season might be four months long and the general election season only two months long. It would be foolish to wait to win the primary, for instance, before knocking on doors of all registered voters in your opponent's party.

If your state has open primaries, once again knock on every door of registered voters despite their declared party. In the same manner, when you are canvassing for the general election you'll need to knock on the doors of all registered voters.

Be organized. I had a Voters Walk List printed out by street, odd and even house numbers and name. Sometimes I walked with a few people from my campaign committee, or I walked with other candidates on my ticket. When we went as a group, we maximized our time by having literature with our ticket printed on them with everyone's name and office they were running for. We would work in teams leapfrogging every other house on the list up and down and across streets.

After every conversation, I ranked the voter 1 to 4 from definitely voting for me to definitely *not* voting for me. Quick in the moment tallies enabled me to designate who I would contact again through a postcard or a phone call. It provided me with a list of who my "definites" were that I could then track on Election Day to be sure they got out to vote. More detailed information on the techniques of knocking on doors is in the Chapter: *Door-to-Door Canvass.*

Analyze who to see when for maximum impact. Obviously, there is a reason to canvass for six to seven months. First, you want to connect with voters personally and make the case why you're their candidate. To maximize your time think about canvassing neighborhoods with a high senior population during the day. And canvass in neighborhoods, where there are working couples, in the evenings or weekends. I walked neighborhoods with driveways or sizeable front yards early in the campaign while I had time on my side. I heard more than once, "You're the first candidate that has ever come to our door."

Towards the end of the campaign when you are working furiously for the commitment of more voters is when it makes the most sense to go through townhome communities and closely spaced individual homes. It's also possible that there are other factors for consideration in your campaign for who you see early and who you see later. Focus on making the strongest impact to seal the votes you need to be elected.

When I ran for the House of Delegates, I went to every home of a registered Democrat first with a volunteer who would work the Voter's List and a piece of campaign literature. Then as my opponents started door knocking, I would appear a second time with a different piece of literature. Near the election, I appeared a final time – by this point, many of the voters were impressed at how hard I was working to secure their vote and my passion for wanting to represent them.

9 WORK THE NUMBERS

B e smart and do the math. In the early days of your campaign take the time to analyze previous election results for the office you are seeking. The information you need is available at your local Election Board/ Election Authority office. It's also possible that the information is readily available on their website or the State's Election Authority website. Gather the results going back two or three elections.

The goal is to create an accurate analysis of how many votes in your district are needed to win the primary *and* the general election. Another factor to consider in the analysis is if you have tough opposition in the primary or general election or if you have a tough battle in both. Knowing how many votes are needed will prevent you from shooting in the dark and will allow you the opportunity to know where you stand as you actively campaign.

For example, if you are running for a State Legislative Office, determine the number of people represented by that office and the number of registered voters for that office's district. If the legislative district has a population of 125,000 people with 100,000 of voting age and voter registration is 70% you will know that there are 70,000 voters. Then go one step further. You're a Democrat, and the district has 45% Democratic voter registration. That results in 31,500 voters who presumably could turn out to vote in the race in a closed primary. But of course, not all registered voters actively vote.

Next step with this same scenario is to analyze voter turnout. If in previous primaries, turnout was 40% of registered Democrats, you are campaigning for 12,600 voters. Against one opponent, it takes 6,301 votes to win. *Your goal is to identify, connect with and get 6,301 of your voters to the polls to vote for you.* You do not need to reach and win over, all 70,000 voters. And if there is more than one opponent you can win with a smaller plurality.

Estimating turnout can be a challenge, but it's also an important part of the equation. Consider the other candidates running in that election. Are there compelling issues in the community that are likely to bring voters to the polls? Once you consider these mitigating factors, you will have to guesstimate if you can "count on" for instance, a 30% or 40% voter turnout.

Obtaining and analyzing the voting history of your district is essential to understand how you will need to spend your resources. If the Democratic Candidate always wins the district, for example, you will know that spending most all your resources in the primary are fine. If the seat that you are running for has gone Democratic and Republican at times, you must have enough resources to fight two campaign battles--- the primary and the general election.

On the other hand, if you are running in an election with no serious opponent in the primary but expect a tough race in the general election; you should campaign in the primary by going to every house where people are registered and asking people to vote for you in the upcoming primary and general election. In a tight race, you can't afford to wait until the primaries are over to reach Independents or Republican voters.

Furthermore, the analysis will reveal that if you have a tough primary election and an easy general election you need to put resources and energy into getting 51% of the expected primary turnout.

If your analysis concludes that you have a tough primary *and* a tough general with serious opponents in both, you need to concentrate on winning the primary. Without a first win, there is no general election for you. As a first time candidate, you may find yourself without much support from fellow party members who are also running. However, once you win the primary, it's time if at all possible to "get along" with the other nominees from your party. If you can work together and run as a unity party ticket for the general election, your campaign resources will easily go further.

If you are running in a state or for an office which has an open primary the analysis of the election history can be more complicated. You have to determine the likelihood and quantity of voters who may cross over from the other parties as well as independent voters. For instance, if the history shows that only a few voters crossed over, then campaign as if the campaign is a closed primary encouraging a few along the way to cross over party lines and vote for you.

On the other hand, if the history shows that the number of voters crossing over party lines or independents voting with your party is high, then you must run the race with the goal of reaching all likely voters in the primary and general elections.

In summary, the point is to find how many votes you need to win each race and gear your campaign to winning those votes. You don't need to talk to every citizen or even every voter. Your focus must be to find and turn out a majority or plurality of voters in the primary and for the general election which in the example above is 6,301 voters in the primary to win. If the general election is expected to have a 60% turnout (42,000 voters), then you will need 21,001 votes in the general election to win.

10 RAISING AN ARMY

Running for a local office such as the City or County Council or The State Legislature usually requires a large number of volunteers. Only in a few lucky scenarios can a candidate be elected without the hard work of volunteers. In fact, I served in the legislature with a politician who spent very little money and did not have volunteers working for him. For example, if you are running unopposed, or if there is a new district as a result of re-districting and you are very well known while your opponent is not, or if an incumbent dies or retires and you are running without a formidable opponent. However, in most situations how effective you are at raising an army of volunteers will impact the outcome of a political bid for a local office.

If you are known for your work in the community, you already have earned the respect of many people. And in fact, these people will be the basis of your army of volunteers. Seek out your friends and associates who have worked with you in the PTA, the Homeowners Association, Recreation and Parks or any of the other groups where you have worked in your community. Solicit their support early on and use them to help you network with additional groups where they have involvement. Keep in mind these people share your vision and are involved in making their community better. Who better than to support you as a candidate running for a local office than people like you?

First, identify your closest supporters. *These are the folks who were genuinely excited when you mentioned wanting to run for office.* They share your enthusiasm for improving the community. These are the folks you want to ask to buy tickets to fundraisers such as cocktail parties or dinners. You might ask them to host an event in their home to introduce you to neighbors or their friends within the district.

Political clubs where you are active will also be a great resource for like-minded people to recruit for your army of volunteers. Also, consider the people who worked with you on an issue to better the community (for me it was the Stop the Highway Committee).

Reach out to college students looking for the experience of working on a local campaign. Retired folks are often looking for ways to contribute to their community. Neighbors recovering from an illness, unemployed people looking to be busy and meet people within the community are all possibilities for your volunteers. Also don't overlook relatives, whether immediate family or second cousins, people become genuinely excited about family members running for office.

Whenever someone volunteers to help with the campaign, ask them to put a bumper sticker on their car or a sign on their lawn. Your name recognition will grow, especially as an "endorsement" from a neighbor.

Match Volunteers to the Job

There are many jobs to do, and there are never enough people to do them all. As a candidate, you will be the primary source of recruiting though hopefully not the only one to recruit. Depending on the size of the campaign you will have an Office Manager and/or a Campaign Manager who must match the right person with the right job. The candidate should not be directly involved with this task; you must devote your time out among the voters.

Some supporters are better working in the campaign office stuffing envelopes or calling voters on the phone to raise money, selling tickets to fundraisers or calling voters that can't be reached easily through a door-to-door canvass. Events such as cocktail parties or dinners will need to be planned including venue, food, drinks, etc. Someone will need to reach out to possible supporters who may be in a position to donate food, drinks or supplies.

Maximizing Your Volunteers

One of the most important volunteer jobs will be preparing the walk list for door-to-door campaigning as well as the job of walking with you door-to-door talking with voters.

While door-to-door campaigning is essential when trying to meet and reach voters, imagine the power that comes with working a particular street with one of your volunteers standing with you who also lives on that street, has a yard sign and now is introducing you to their neighbors as their choice for the office.

Someone who is willing to walk the community and introduce you to neighbors might also be a good source for hosting an evening coffee or tea. As the candidate, you attend with a ten-minute presentation and answer questions. And finally, before leaving you ask people in attendance to take yard signs and bumper stickers.

(For more details regarding maximizing an evening coffee or tea event refer to Chapter: *Neighborhood Coffees & Teas).*

At your fundraiser cocktail party or dinner for your campaign, ask your volunteers who may be directing people for parking or acting as greeters, about asking attendees for permission to place a bumper sticker on their car. Whenever possible, have the volunteer *place the bumper sticker on the car.* It's the foolproof way to be sure it does make it onto the car. Also, ask attendees to leave with yard signs in the same manner as suggested for a coffee or tea. The more signs and bumper stickers are seen throughout the community, the stronger you appear as a serious candidate worthy of a vote even among voters who you have yet to connect with directly.

How Many Volunteers Will I Need?

It's important to note that the recruiting of volunteers will be necessary throughout the campaign. If you are running an effective local campaign, you will always be recruiting. To keep recruiting is to keep firing up your voters, so they want to vote for you, and they want their families and friends to vote for you too. You need as many volunteers as possible.

The bigger the campaign, the bigger the army of volunteers needed. In addition to having the volunteers be suited for the best job possible to keep them engaged, keep in mind that some volunteers will give many hours and other will give a few. In addition to needing as many helping hands as possible, look at every volunteer involvement as the opportunity to seal a vote. No one is more committed than someone who has given their time and effort to help a candidate win an election. And not only can you count on that person's vote, but think of them as ambassadors in the community. The likelihood is that they will share with their relatives, neighbors, and co-workers that they are volunteering for your campaign. As a candidate, having voters speak of their commitment to working to get you elected is priceless.

Encourage your volunteers and thank them profusely. Every contribution from a volunteer no matter how small is valuable. For all the reasons cited above its imperative that they believe they are a part of something good. Some volunteers will disappoint you; others will surprise you. All need to be thanked and to feel appreciated. Campaign volunteers are not employees. Encourage your volunteers, expect the most and be thrilled with anything they contribute.

11 RUTHLESS EFFICIENCY

"What you are doing for the next minute, how you are spending the next dollar, must relate to getting a vote or don't do it."
    --Tim Hickman

I have seen candidates waste an inordinate amount of time and money while campaigning. For this reason, the statement above became my mantra.

I have witnessed candidates and campaign supporters spending ridiculous amounts of time, plotting and scheming on how to lash out at the opposition. I have seen campaign workers spending far too much time on analyzing the circumstances of their candidates' run for office in comparison to the opposition. All the while they were missing opportunities to use their resources and energy to connect with the voters.

I have also seen candidates waste valuable time at events or door knocking speaking with a voter at great length. Once a voter assures you that they are voting for you, thank them and walk away. Your time is better spent working for the next vote. And even when you have not been promised the vote, your interaction needs to be brief and to the point. It's imperative to get in front of as many voters as possible: state your name, the office you're seeking, why you're running and ask them for their vote.

There are also candidates or campaign managers who make a mistake and purchase elaborate tri-fold brochures or postcards in the heaviest card stock available. Thinking they can win more votes by an impressive well-produced mail piece when it's wiser to price out a variety of brochures and postcards. Direct mail pieces need to be color, heavy enough stock not to fold easily in the mail with a well thought out message. This same brochure or postcard can be edited a few times slightly or perhaps used with different pictures to keep it fresh and ultimately be mailed occasionally throughout the campaign. It behooves you to use your campaign funds efficiently and reach out to voters more frequently than buying top of the line direct mail pieces with the intent of fewer mailings.

It's extremely important to trust your Treasurer and Campaign Committee. They need to respect the efficiency in which you need to manage your campaign funds and use your volunteer staff. I met with them and other candidates I was running with regularly. However, I met with the Office Manager every morning to review the day's agenda and answer any questions regarding expenditures or tasks for them or the volunteers.

It's tempting to sit in the office and "manage" the campaign, but it's neither efficient nor effective. I started every day in the office, but once 10 am rolled around, I was out the door with a few volunteers. We canvassed from 10 am to dusk seven days a week without exemption. I wrapped the day up and was back in the office following any evening events such as coffees or teas. I fell into bed by 11:00 or 12:00 woke up and started the next day in the same way all over again.

12 CAMPAIGN LITERATURE & PROMOTIONAL MATERIAL

Campaign Stationery & Business Cards

As with everything in a campaign, it's important to make every dollar count when printing campaign literature or other campaign collateral. One of the first tasks after you declare your candidacy is to create professional stationery. You will need letterhead when you write letters to voters, when responding to questionnaires, when writing letters to the local newspapers or a letter to the editor. You will also use stationery when you're selling tickets to fundraisers.

In addition, you'll use the stationery for target mailings to organizations or fellow activists who worked on a community issue or people who signed a petition. In targeted letters on stationery, you have the opportunity to connect with voters and create an intimate forum to express why you're running and how you and the voter share an opinion or stand on a particular issue.

For instance, imagine the power of a letter on your stationery to a bike club. You mention in the letter where you bicycle and you specifically mention your commitment to creating a safe bike trail in the community. Take this one step further and connect with *every* bike club that may exist in your district. If you're committed to saving a park, then connect with every environmental group in your district and use your stationery to write a letter stating your commitment to this issue and asking for their vote. When I met with organizations that were uncomfortable giving us names and addresses of their members, we asked if we could supply the letters, stamps and envelopes if they would mail them on behalf of our campaign. It was particularly important if the group endorsed our campaign to find ways to reach their members.

In addition, have business cards printed with your name, the office you are running for and any pertinent campaign information, especially the website. You'll find dozens of ways to use the business cards, but most importantly you will always have something with you while you are out and about in your community. In particular, business cards are useful until your literature is printed and the campaign is in full swing.

Brochures

Campaign literature can take many forms including letters to voters, postcards, to a palm card (think vertical card) which can offer the candidate's name, a slogan with a short bio and a couple of photographs. The size is approximately 4"x8," and it also is known in the business as a rack card.

At the beginning of the campaign after filing as a candidate, and before printing my brochures, I utilized my announcement press release with a photograph as my brochure. It was an 8.5" x 11" sheet of paper. While it was far from my main campaign brochures, the point here is that I didn't wait. Once I filed, I started campaigning in earnest.

My favorite piece of campaign literature, however, is what was known as an "action brochure." It was a very large piece of paper which measured 19" x 16.5," and when folded multiple times it was 4.75" x 8.75". In our case, the front image was the team walking down the street with the names of the candidates printed beneath the photo. On the back of the brochure, the names were printed prominently almost resembling a bumper sticker. Inside each folded panel each candidate had their photograph and biography. In our brochure, we had the State Senator and his bio, and then the candidate for County Council and that bio. The next fold had four panels dedicated to each of the three candidates running for the Lower House of The State Legislature. The last panel consisted of the party's Central Committee. These five candidates had a smaller photograph along with their biography.

On the inside of the brochure were photos of the candidates and issue statements. For instance, we had a picture of a bulldozer in front of highway construction. Then we wrote how we fought and would continue to fight against the expansion of the highway in our community followed by bullet points. In another photograph, we featured candidates talking with a police officer, followed by our stand on law enforcement. There was a picture of the park with bullet points on our stance on the environment. The piece was not folded evenly so that the bottom 1" of the inside showed with our slogan on it, intended to encourage readers to open the brochure.

When I canvassed as part of a team, we would leave this brochure with the voter as well as when no one answered the door. I wrote: *Sorry I missed you,* with my signature. These pieces were signed before we canvassed door-to-door. I carefully tucked the brochure in the door, so the brochure back was revealing our names and the offices we were seeking.

Printing an action brochure such as the one described is expensive and time-consuming. I had professional photographers who volunteered to work on the brochure alongside graphic designers who also volunteered for the campaign. As a candidate supported by local unions, it was important to have the "union bug" appear in fine print on the brochure. A union bug is a small printers' union logo.

On one occasion, much to my regret, I paid a local graphic designer & typesetter to create the layout and print the brochure. What I discovered after the printing of our brochures is that the typesetter allowed our opponents to copy the design *exactly.* There were different photos and candidates, but the layout was identical. It turned out the typesetter supported our opponents. It was a painful lesson where I learned how vital it is to keep as much as you can close to your chest and be very careful when you need to reach beyond your supporters and volunteers for campaign business.

Also, when you come up with a winning design, modify it for use in a variety of purposes. While the action brochure was my favorite as it informed our voters thoroughly, we also used it to mail voters in the district. By shrinking the size of the font on a back panel that listed all our names, we were able to have it addressed to our voting families with a Bulk Rate Permit. We planned for it to be received a few weeks before the election.

We canvassed every home in the district two and a half times. The "half" were high density, easy to walk, townhome communities. We printed many of the mailing versions of the brochure as described above and it had a different cover and back. As a result, when we canvassed a second or third time the brochure looked a little different. While your message and stand on the issues is the same, you want the brochure to look different to increase the likelihood a voter will read it.

Additionally, I dissected the design used for my brochure so that those creative elements could also be used for print ads in local publications, fliers for speaking engagements, etc. If you have a volunteer who is a graphic artist or versed in Photoshop, this will prove especially helpful. It is vital that graphically all your campaign literature is consistent in colors, layout and overall look because you want voters to visibly recognize your campaign literature before they see your name on it!

Sample Ballots

Sample ballots are a palm card handed out at the polls on Election Day. It can be a one-sided card with the names of the candidate or candidates. We used the same graphic design and color scheme as we used in the printed brochures.

Another version of the sample ballot is the same size as the palm card with your name or a list of names on the cover but opens up with an exact reproduction of what voters will see Election Day on the paper ballot, touch screen, punch card or election machine.

Particularly if your Election Board/Election Authority does not mail a sample or specimen ballot to every voter, it is useful and appreciated by the voter to receive in the mail a sample or specimen ballot a week or two before the election. But this does not preclude it from being handed out at the polls. Print it with your name and the names on your ticket if you're running with other candidates, and include the names of all the other candidates running including your opponents.

What? Your opponents name and place on the ballot mailed to every voter? Yes – Many voters like to mark up a ballot at home and take it to the polls with them. If they take yours, they may vote for you or some of your supported candidates. Although the opponents names are on there, darken your name (and your teams' names) print them bold and circle them while the opposition is paler, faded gray and not as readable.

The sample ballot is not meant to do what a brochure does because at best a voter will just glance at it. If you are running with candidates for a lesser position their name on your sample ballot will give them a boost. In essence, they're riding on your coattails. In the same manner, you can also receive a boost Election Day if your name is on a sample ballot of a higher, more visible or popular office seeker. However, be aware this can present a problem too. If the candidate of a higher office is losing the race, you will want those voting against him to still vote for you.

Postcards

Postcards provide an opportunity to extract parts of the brochure for a less expensive mailing than the brochure. We also printed over 10,000 personal endorsement postcards to accompany the coffees and teas we held throughout the campaign. The strategy and design of the postcards are described in detail in the Chapter: *Neighborhood Coffees and Teas.*

In addition to what we used at coffee and teas, we asked campaign volunteers, supporters, friends, families, and colleagues to address personal endorsement postcards to their circles of friends, families, coworkers, and neighbors in the district.

Bumper Stickers

While I encourage you to create tasteful campaign literature and signage pleasing to voters for their graphic appeal and message, these rules *do not* apply to bumper stickers. I insisted our yard signs be tasteful and labored over color and fonts. However, I wanted the bumper stickers to pop. It is important for bumper stickers to be seen in an instant when cars are in motion as well as parked.

Bumper stickers are competing with an incredible amount of stimuli confronting drivers, and they must be recognized and read quickly. My choice for the bumper stickers was a fluorescent yellow with black lettering. It was bright, easily recognizable and seen in the day or night.

What should you print on a bumper sticker? Just as you want the color to pop on a bumper sticker, the same goes for the message. It should contain a minimal amount of information. First, the candidate's name as large as possible and in smaller type your party and office you are seeking. You are also required to print an authority line although it can be printed very small. Lastly, if you are seeking union endorsements or votes by the members of unions print your bumper stickers along with your other literature in a union shop, and have the union bug printed in very small type on the bumper stickers.

How many bumper stickers to order? In a very small race, you may need only 250. The races I ran in I ordered 500 – 1000. Everyone you know should have a bumper sticker: family, friends, and volunteers, people who work with you in business or the community. There are paper and plastic bumper stickers. Plastic is more expensive but is more easily removable after the election. For people reluctant to put bumper stickers on their car, we offered to remove them after the election. Some folks taped them inside the back window. Small magnetic signs taking the place of bumper stickers have become popular in elections although they are much more expensive. On the other hand, if it allows more people willing to put a "bumper sticker" on their car it may be worth the expense.

Yard Signs

There are many factors for effectively using yard signs for your campaign. While it's important to consider the overall cost of the signs, you must decide where you can benefit from signs, the quantity you'll need for large and small signs, and the effect weather will have on the material you choose.

Signs can be constructed using cardboard or vinyl. While cardboard signs are less expensive, they don't stand up to weather as well as vinyl. You can also purchase waxed cardboard signs which make them less vulnerable to weather. Signs can also be constructed using a thin plastic vinyl that slips over a metal frame. Finally, there are plastic signs that are corrugated similar to corrugated cardboard which is the most expensive and the most durable. And while the cardboard signs need to be attached to lumber, the corrugated plastic signs have a metal posts with prongs that slide up into the sign and likewise into the ground.

We salvaged wood from a discarded picket fence for our large cardboard signs. We stapled the cardboard signs to the lumber and used at least one piece of the wood for the crosspiece to prevent the sign from curling up. We also learned from experience that it was necessary to hammer the wood into the ground and then staple the sign to the wood after hammering or it rips the cardboard. There is no reason not to have a combination of plastic and cardboard signs as long as the overall look is identical. Lastly, be sure to consider signs where you can benefit from a two-sided sign such as what you'll need for a street corner and locations where one side will suffice.

Also, give some thought to the look and the message of the signs. What is the primary message on the signs that you want voters to see while passing? Consider the colors you choose and the readability of the signs. Can passers-by read your signs from a distance? We chose earth tones with the belief that supporters would be more likely to embrace the signs on their front lawns. Whatever you choose for colors, font and message, be consistent.

However, as the candidate, I urge you to make certain that your supporters have acquired all the necessary approvals before erecting a sign. If a sign is erected without the proper permission or worse is on public property, you can be sure your opponent will make it a campaign issue.

Large signs are an effective way to utilize high traffic areas such as busy intersections or an empty lot owned by a supporter. Large yard signs act as a billboard; they will be seen by many voters but at a fraction of the cost of a billboard.

While large signs are important to your campaign, yard signs are equally as important. There is nothing as impressive as driving through a neighborhood peppered with your signs. What better statement for a voter than to drive through their neighborhood and see that many of their neighbors are supporting you?

It was powerful for me as a candidate to drive down a street and see 20-yard signs in a community of 40 houses. Knocking on doors in such a neighborhood was exhilarating. In the same manner, it was depressing to canvass in a neighborhood filled with my opponents' signs. That's why it's important to ask family members, friends, volunteers and as many willing voters as possible, to place a sign in their yard. We particularly worked very hard to find sign placement opportunities on high traffic streets.

One final word on yard signs: sign maintenance. It is imperative to have a couple of volunteers dedicated to sign maintenance. There are often supporters of both sides in an election who may make a game out of vandalizing signs. We urged our supporters not to destroy our opponents' signs even if the other side had destroyed some of our signs.

Be aware that sometimes political signs are targeted by neighborhood vandals. In fact, we often asked supporters to take our signs down over Halloween and erect them again after the holiday. In any event, it was necessary to have a couple of people assigned to riding around and repairing or replacing our signs as they became damaged.

Signs and More "Signs"

Billboards allow you the opportunity to capture the attention of many voters in your district, but often they are prohibitively expensive. It's important to weigh the probability that many of the people passing the billboard are voters in your district vs. the cost of the billboard.

On the other hand, supporters who are willing to allow a large sign on their lot or at a busy intersection are making a strong statement of support and providing an opportunity to be in front of many voters. In fact, give thought early on to the busiest intersections in your district and how best to capitalize on these high traffic areas. Whether through a billboard or connecting with the owner of the lot or house, it may go a long way in getting your name out among voters.

And just as supporters who are willing to allow a large sign on their lot or at a busy intersection are instrumental in helping you be in front of voters, so is having a sign that is either silk-screened or hand painted in the window of a local business. We also had a few of these signs in townhome windows. There were signs made for cars which became "portable billboards." You may want to consider car toppers that look like pizza driver tops as another way to have your message "move" through the community.

Campaign buttons are useful for identifying you as the candidate whether you're at the grocery store or campaigning door-to-door. Your family members and your closest supporters will wear campaign buttons. They are useful for volunteers working for you and at rallies or special events. Be warned, however, that most of the time buttons end up in the sock drawer.

When I ran as part of a team, I had 3" buttons made that featured the whole team. On another occasion, I had a 1.25" button that featured my name and the office I was seeking. Buttons are helpful for name recognition but like all dollars spent during a campaign, be careful of spending too much money on something that may only be moderately helpful in getting your name out among voters.

Balloons are a fun giveaway for family picnic days or a 4th of July parade. We rented a helium tank and had our volunteers blowing up balloons and handing them out along the parade route to kids waiting with their parents for the parade to begin. As I walked the parade route, it was uplifting to see families in the community enjoying the parade while many balloons with my name and the office I was running for were lining the parade route.

Candidates can also use cardboard sunscreens for cars depending on the climate. The new re-usable cloth grocery bags are another idea for reaching voters with your name and desired office on it. One less common giveaway by a candidate running for Attorney General was a nail file with his name on it. He gave so many of these away that it became a running joke that *everyone* had at least one.

These are all ideas of how to reinforce the door-to-door canvass, the meeting, and greeting at workplaces, grocery stores and the like.

As a candidate, you need to balance cost effectiveness with the opportunity to reach more voters. And while there are many clever ways to get your name out, I found large and small yard signs and bumper stickers were cost effective and the best way to reach the most potential voters in the community. However, all the ideas shared here are intended to reinforce not replace the face to face contact you the candidate have had as you canvass the neighborhoods in your district.

13 ACTIVITIES AT CAMPAIGN HEADQUARTERS

Your campaign headquarters will be the home base for everything from meetings with your Campaign Committee, to catching up on paperwork such as questionnaires, to meetings with media, to fundraising activities and so much more. At the heart of much of the activity will be the Office Manager who will deal with walk-ins, remind you of tasks and deadlines and most important of all organize the variety of tasks that need to be performed with help from your volunteers.

In fact, the Office Manager is the primary person to direct your volunteers. In preparation for each day's door-to-door canvass, you will need volunteers to prepare the folder with the walk list information. This task will be performed using political campaign software such as VoteBuilder/VAN or manually from the Voters List. For more of the preparation and process refer to the Chapter: *Door-to-Door Canvass.*

Print mailing labels from your political campaign software or the Voters List. Labels are printed dependent on the election at hand: in an open primary or general election, you send the direct mail pieces to all the voters in the district while in a closed primary mail only to members of the party. If two or more voters were at the same address, we had a label with "Ed and Jo Ellen" or the "Hopkins family." We printed a shared label for two or more residents of a household of a similar age to save on the number of direct mail pieces per household. However, if a much younger voter resided at the same address, with particularly older voters, we mailed another direct mail piece to that person.

Another very important task for the Office Manager is to assist and coordinate the volunteer army in sending the many mailings out. This was particularly challenging for the broad mailings that were sent to all of our party voters in the district. Once the labels were printed the Office Manager with possible help from the candidate and other members of the committee, worked to bring in a large group of volunteers for a couple of evenings. We provided drinks and snacks and tried to make it a party atmosphere. Large folding tables were set up, and our volunteers worked stuffing envelopes, attaching labels or doing both. We were able to prepare 30,000 pieces for mailing in 2 nights.

Another major consideration before any mailing is how to best mail your direct mail piece. For instance, a brochure will be different than an oversized postcard. Post office regulations often change, so it's important to find out the rules to maximize the efficiency of both cost and timeliness. There are various ways to presort the mail to save money. However, one thing for certain: the more sorting performed on your end, the less expensive the mailing will be. It's best to check with the USPS in your area to find out what works best for your campaign.

Regardless of how you mail your various direct mail pieces, you will need to buy a Standard/Bulk Rate Permit for a year. Time the purchase if possible to include both the primary and general elections.

When we prepared our mailings for the USPS, we loaded up several cars with the mail and drove to the main post office in the city and met with the director of bulk mail. When we specified this was a political mailing they marked the bags with a red tag that specified "political campaign mailing." While the USPS offers no guarantee as to delivery time, they are processed like first class. *In other words, the bags were marked as Bulk Rate but processed as first class.* The thought behind it is the postal service does not want to deliver one candidate's mail over another into the homes faster. Regular bulk mail allows a much greater window for delivery than first class.

If you can afford it, the high quantity mailings, can be handled efficiently by employing a mail house that will apply postage, addresses, and mail the pieces directly. That said, it would be advisable to receive a few quotes to be sure it is cost effective. Part of this equation will be the size of your volunteer army. If you don't have enough volunteers, it may be impossible to have a mass mailing done without employing a mail house to label and apply postage.

We also conducted many personalized mailings from our headquarters. While the Office Manager did not have to recruit dozens of volunteers to help as was necessary with a district-wide mailing, we still counted on the support of volunteers. For example, we had mailings of postcards from the many teas we held. We thought they needed first class stamps. A candidate I ran with had the Recreational Council mailing list, so we proposed a separate mailing for that list promoting our team of candidates.

We regularly purchased an update of new registrants and had volunteers stuff a letter signed by me that welcomed the new voter and inserted a brochure and mailed both to them. While a district-wide mailing occurred two or three times within a campaign, I mailed to new registrants who either just moved in or became of voting age every couple of weeks. Whenever we were able to reach a particular group in our district through a personalized mailing, we did it.

In addition to the mailings, campaign headquarters was home to volunteers calling voters, preparing walk lists, fundraising business, and much more.

14 THE DAILY SCHEDULE

D iscipline is the key to maintaining a daily schedule where you canvass door-to-door every day. It's grueling hard work, and it still is the most effective way to get in front of voters and win their support. I began the door-to-door canvass five months before the primary and I didn't miss a single day.

I began each day in the office at 7 or 8 am. This time was spent meeting with the Office Manager, responding to surveys and endorsement questionnaires, working on press releases, and reviewing the activities of the day including how to maximize our volunteers. We also prepared our walk list to utilize our time canvassing. However, my absolute rule, no matter what office chores needed attention, was to be out the door and on the street by 10 am. I canvassed in the morning and afternoon by myself or with a small group of people.

I door knocked until 1 or 2 pm and then would take a half hour break for lunch. I then resumed door-to-door canvassing until a dinner break at 4:30 or 5:00. If it was summer, I would take a quick shower, eat a nutritious dinner with protein and be back out at 5:30 or 6 when folks were home from work. When I canvassed in the evening, during the general election, I canvassed with other candidates running on the ticket.

I concluded the door-to-door canvass at dusk. People are reluctant to open their door as the sun begins to set. However, as a candidate, your day is not over. It's either back to the office to work on paperwork left unfinished when you started canvassing earlier in the day, check up on the volunteers, strategize with other candidates if running on a ticket, or you're off to a neighborhood coffee and tea. It's also possible that you'll need to do both—attend a neighborhood tea and then return to the office.

15 THE DOOR-TO-DOOR CANVASS

here are candidates who think they are campaigning by having a team of volunteers walk through a community for a "lit drop" in every door of a neighborhood, or every door of registered voters by referring to the Voters List. *Nothing replaces knocking on a door and humbly standing before a voter and asking for their support.* In my district of 125,000, my team and I knocked on every door of a registered party voter two and a half times.

The only exception to the use of a lit drop is near the end of a campaign. For instance, you have 3,000 pieces of campaign literature left and some volunteers who while eager to work for you, are perhaps too inexperienced to door knock and engage voters. Campaign literature is useless sitting in a box. Instead, blitz a neighborhood or two as a reminder to vote.

Preparation is Key

Before you begin knocking on doors, as with every other step mentioned in campaigning, it's best to prepare. The more you prepare, the more efficient your door-to-door canvass will be.

When I first campaigned, I wore dress shoes with heavy leather soles and wore them out the first month. Then I noticed what the mail carrier wore and I invested in a pair of shoes that resembled dress shoes at first glance but had thick, soft rubber soles. They didn't wear out as easily, and they were much kinder to my feet and legs. Dress as you would if you were going to work in an office. If you're walking with volunteers, they don't need to wear a tie or be particularly dressed up but request they wear business casual. However, as a candidate standing before voters, you must look the part.

Walking List for the Canvass

Technological advances allow a candidate the opportunity to save time and be more efficient in preparing the walk list for the door-to-door canvass. However, it needs to make sense for the office you are seeking and the number of voters you need to reach.

Campaign software such as VoteBuilder/VAN can create walk lists with detailed demographic information and phone numbers included. The walk list is folder ready as it provides the opportunity to draw your canvassing turf for that day. The person that builds the walk list ("cut turf") must be a savvy, well-trained staff member or volunteer that understands the software.

Alternatively, you can purchase a Voters List from your Election Authority. They may provide it organized by street, and house numbers, odd and even. If not you will have to pay a data center or a programmer to prepare the list and if possible add the phone numbers or your volunteers will need to cross-reference the list with the phone directory later.

If you purchase either an electronic or printed copy of the Voters List, have a campaign volunteer in your office prep it for canvassing. At this point, the list will have been printed out by street with odds and evens separated. You will also have obtained from the election office maps with boundary lines of your district for the office you are seeking. If your local election office doesn't offer maps showing district lines, they will provide you the boundaries, and you need to have the boundaries applied to local street maps. Don't assume you know the boundaries, have it verified.

Next, the volunteers will need to make multiple copies of the map. Before a day's canvass, they should staple or glue the map to the inside of a folder with the Voters List. On the map, will be a highlighted path that you will walk to canvass. For example, it may have you walking down one side of the street back up the other side taking a detour down a cul-de-sac continuing walking around the corner, to another street, returning eventually to finish the second side of the second street and back to your car. The trick is to minimize the walking as much as possible so you can maximize time spent door knocking. Of course, if you live in a district in a rural area or where the lawns are expansive you will want to do the same thing while driving from house to house.

Whether you are using campaign software like VAN to prepare the walk list or using the Voters List to prepare the days canvass, consider the topology of the neighborhood. I found it best to knock off townhomes in the evening when more voters were home and larger homes with large lawns earlier in the day. Be considerate and don't cut across lawns no matter how tempting. Consider valleys where streets become darker earlier: you do not want to knock on a door and find yourself standing in the dark.

Finally, when you consider the path for canvassing, also consider the demographics of the neighborhoods. If there is a neighborhood in your district where many retired people live, for instance, that becomes a perfect target for a daytime canvass.

Apartments are another consideration. I found some complexes to be very transient. As a result, the Voters List had an inaccurate record of voters many whom previously lived in the apartment.

And remember, as Election Day draws near, and you are repeating the door-to-canvass, it's time to re-visit the high yield neighborhoods such as townhouses where you can be in front of as many voters as possible. I also recommend you repeat the canvass of the neighborhoods where you feel an affinity as "your voters" rather than your opponents'. The goal here is to maximize your turnout.

General Tips for Door Knocking

Introduce yourself, the office you are seeking, the reason you are running and ask for their vote.

Examples of Introduction:

Hi, I'm Nora Sanders. I'm running for County Council. I live in this community, and I believe our community needs a voice. I'm asking for your vote.

Hi, I'm Nora Sanders. I'm running for County Council. I grew up in this community, and I believe our community needs a voice. I'm asking for your vote.

Hi, I'm Nora Sanders. I'm running for County Council. I went to school in this community, and I believe our community needs a voice. I'm asking for your vote.

Hi, I'm Nora Sanders. I'm running for County Council. I live in this neighborhood, and I believe our community needs a voice. I'm asking for your vote.

Hi, I'm Nora Sanders. I'm running for County Council. I believe politics can be an honorable profession and I'm asking for your vote.

Hi, I'm Nora Sanders. I'm running for County Council. I believe we need a change in (name the county seat) and I'm asking for your vote.

It's important to be brief and to the point and most of all as a candidate, you must make a connection to the voter at the door. If the connection is personal, (school, grew up, etc.), that's even better. And of course, handing your literature in hopes of resonating with that voter is essential.

It's most helpful if you can canvass with someone from the neighborhood who can introduce you to neighbors as a personal endorsement. If you don't have a volunteer from the neighborhood to join you, it's useful to canvass with a volunteer or two to keep your spirits up.

I also had student volunteers from time to time who would work the Walk List for me as we canvassed. Rather than me looking at paper and walking and door knocking, they would be looking at the list ahead of me. I introduced myself to a voter while they were planning the next stop. They could then tell me, for instance in the primary, to knock on #12 telling me that there are three Jones in the house, but only Carter, 23 years old, is registered to our party. If Carter wasn't home, I would ask the woman who answered, (presumably his Mom), to give Carter our literature and tell him I'm hoping he will consider me for the Democratic primary. And in such a situation, it didn't hurt to add that I hoped she and her husband would consider me in the general election.

There will be times when it seems that no one is home. When I wasn't having much luck in the daytime and was working with two or three volunteers, I asked them to walk ahead ringing doorbells and knocking on doors still referring to the Walk List. When they engaged someone at the door, I stepped onto the porch and introduced myself. My volunteers assisted me in covering neighborhoods faster. This method was especially useful early on in the campaign.

One technique that is especially helpful if you are running as part of a ticket is to canvass door-to-door as a team. For instance, I ran with five candidates: three for the lower house Legislature, one for the Senate, and one for County Council. We canvassed together leapfrogging each other, and when someone answered a door, I introduced myself and the office I was seeking and then pointed and named the other candidates and the offices they were seeking. If they noticed I had engaged someone at the door, they would wave, or if they were close enough to where I stood, they walked to the door and shook their hand.

It's almost as effective as each individual coming to the door. It also provided us the opportunity to cover more territory quickly to get in front of more voters. As part of a ticket, even when I canvassed on my own I always mentioned the names of the other candidates on the team and expected them to do the same.

Be smart with the time you are in front of voters at their front door. As mentioned earlier, it's a numbers game, and it's essential to be in front of as many voters as possible. *Introduce yourself and the office you are seeking, and why (in a sentence), you are seeking office and ask for their vote.*

I have witnessed candidates who didn't use the information on the Voters List wisely and who engaged voters for fifteen minutes and then would surmise that they either were not registered to vote or were registered with the other party. While wasting those fifteen minutes, I knocked on ten doors and engaged briefly with six voters. In fact, I ran with a candidate who not only spent an inordinate amount of time talking to nonvoters but she was incapable of disengaging from the conversation. If this is an issue for you as a candidate, train your volunteers in the art of politely disengaging for you.

When I knocked on a door looking for a voter from the Walk List and the person answering identified themselves as unregistered, I offered them a registration form with a stamped envelope. Obviously, I had this prepared in advance. Then I gave them my short introductory speech and my campaign literature.

There will be times when you run into a hostile person. A voter who will tell you that he or she believes that "all politicians are crooked and that the system is broken." There were times when I was shouted at or insulted. While unnerving, I found it worked to agree with them (to a degree), and say that's why I'm running. "I'm not crooked, and I believe in democracy, and I'm committed to making a difference. I believe politics can be an honorable profession." Surprisingly, many such people backed down, and there were times they also asked for a bumper sticker or yard sign! And in the situations where I couldn't turn them around, I still felt vindicated and less affected by their negative comments.

In fact, the most memorable story of a hostile encounter involved a heated exchange between a voter and me. (It was a tough day and we volleyed back and forth as to why I was running and his negative views concerning all politicians.) About an hour later he drove around the neighborhood to find me and apologize. On Election Day, I happened to be standing in front of his polling station. My opponent attempted to give him campaign literature. He brusquely pushed him aside and said, "I'm voting for that one," and snatched a ballot out of my hand and walked in to vote. It was a fun experience.

Rate Your Voters

One of the most important functions of the door-to-door canvass is the opportunity to rate your voters as to the likelihood or non-likelihood that you have their vote. It's a component you will need as you near Election Day to know which voters you need to get to the polls and vote for you. It's also a "report card" of how you're doing in the campaign and how many people have committed or are likely to commit to voting for you. We gave voters a rating of 1 to 4. A rating of 1 was a voter that identified themselves as committed to you or was extremely enthusiastic. On Election Day this is a person who one of your volunteers will call or visit to remind them to vote and ask if they need a ride to the polls or a babysitter to enable them to vote etc.

Voters you met at the door that were friendly and receptive you might mark as a 2. These were people who were not totally committed, but you have a hope of persuading them nearer to Election Day whether through mailings or additional door knocking. Voters with a 3 rating are not committed, and you are not sure of how they will vote. Those with a 4 rating lean towards your opponent and may have a yard sign or a car with an opponent's bumper sticker. Voters' houses identified as 4 are not worth going back to---your energy is better spent somewhere else. However, one exception to this rule is if for example, there are multiple voters in the house and there is one car with your opponent's bumper sticker. It is possible that not all voters within the house are voting for your opponent.

Political campaign software such as VoteBuilder/VAN streamlines the voter rating process since the software includes phone numbers. However, there is still a need for data entry for the ratings to become part of the record.

If you're not using political campaign software, and your Voters List does not include phone numbers you'll need your volunteers to find the phone numbers for your 1's and 2's. There are phone directories like the Criss Cross Directory that are available in print and online which provide landline phone numbers by street in house number order like the Voters List.

However, the Criss Cross Directory is only available in some areas. The print version can be found in some public libraries or borrowed from a business. Otherwise, volunteers will have to look up by name those 1's and 2's using a phone directory or alternate technology. Be aware that both Criss Cross and using phone directories online will only identify landlines. While it might be a task for your volunteers to find the phone numbers, it's an important task. It will enable you to have volunteers follow up to encourage these voters to get to the polls. Many elections have been won or lost by a candidate's ability or inability to GOTV (Get Out The Vote).

You can take technology a step further and use a mobile canvassing app such as MiniVAN which allows you to go door-to-door using an Android or iOS smartphone or device eliminating the need for paper folders and maps. In this scenario, all interactions at the door including rating the voter are recorded in real time.

In conclusion, the meticulous preparation and utilization of walk lists for the door-to-door canvass is essential for effectiveness whether your list is generated using campaign software, the Voters List or a mobile canvassing application.

Converting Dog Bites into Votes

Beware of dogs but if you do have the misfortune of being bitten be sure to use it to your maximum advantage. I was bitten three different times while campaigning for a primary. The first time was a small dog in a baby doll dress that bolted out the front door and hooked onto my Achilles tendon. The owner was apologetic and very concerned. The second time was when I walked onto a porch and didn't see the German Shepherd lying beneath the glider. The dog lifted the glider off the ground and latched onto my foot. Gratefully, the dog did not penetrate my shoe.

In the third incident, I was walking down the sidewalk, referring to the Voters List when a Dalmatian collided with me and bit my leg. Again the owner was extremely apologetic and luckily it wasn't a bad bite. However, the result of my three encounters was for the owners to take both yard signs and bumper stickers. It may have been a sympathy vote in all three instances because their dogs had misbehaved, but so be it. I won three more votes.

Another candidate I ran with on a ticket had the misfortune of being chased by a dog after knocking on the first house his first-day campaigning. He knocked on the door, and we heard the dog galloping through the house. As the dog jumped at the door, the glass came out. The candidate was chased on top of a car and was feeding campaign literature to a large dog to keep from being bitten.

After being bitten three times, I began to carry a small folding umbrella in my back pocket. If I was chased again, I planned on putting it in the dog's mouth like a stick in hopes of distracting the dog until his owner could control him.

We did gain valuable insight as to when there could be a problem with a dog. At times it was a gut feeling as to if there was a dog on the property. If there was a fenced yard in the front of the house with a dirt path just inside the fence, we anticipated there was a dog. If there was a chain link fence, we rattled the gate to see if a dog came running. While dogs remain the biggest threat, I was once attacked by a bird when I unknowingly was too close to a nest.

Summary:

Prepare to make the most of your time while canvassing. It's an essential component for getting in front of voters, and it's important to look the part of the candidate and canvass effectively. I canvassed seven days a week for five months, no exceptions. I'm sure I pulled in a few sympathy votes while knocking on doors in the pouring rain. In the heat of summer, I was able to measure the heat by the salt line that formed on my tie from perspiration. I rinsed my ties overnight and dried out my shoes which also turned white from salt. It's physically draining but my diligence with the door-to-door canvass undoubtedly was the difference in the elections I won.

Door-to-Door Canvass Check List
- Comfortable walking shoes
- Water
- Folding Umbrella
- Voting by mail applications and stamps in the case of a voter who will either be away or unable to get to the polls
- Clipboard with voter registration forms with stamps
- Campaign Literature already signed by you, "Sorry I Missed you" for houses where no one was home
- Campaign Literature
- Folders with Voters List, maps and routes highlighted & stapled to inside of folder (each walk list that day for canvassing has its own folder)
- Alternatively, Android or iOS smartphones or tablet set up for MiniVAN or other campaign application with the walk list loaded.

16 NEIGHBORHOOD COFFEES & TEAS

At dusk, door-to-door canvassing has come to a close but campaigning for the day is not over. One of the many important volunteer jobs is to schedule and coordinate people to host coffees, teas, or cocktail hours on your behalf. The goal is to have as many of these gatherings as possible.

These social gatherings are an effective way to connect with voters. When I campaigned, it proved to be a tremendous asset for growing the base of people committed to voting for me and for growing the base of volunteers.

Here is how to maximize your effectiveness at an evening coffee in your district: first, the host or hostess invites neighbors, family and friends to their house with you as the scheduled guest of honor. You arrive with yard signs and bumper stickers and pre-printed postcards with a campaign message. You will address the group, share your vision including why you're running for office and your commitment to making a difference in local government. As a candidate, it's important to listen and address their concerns for the community.

In closing the evening, you will ask for their support in the way of voting, volunteering or helping to spread the word among their friends and neighbors within your district. Ask if anyone will put a yard sign in front of their house or be willing to take a bumper sticker for their car. Your mission is not only to get the commitment of the voters in the room but to get them fired up enough to help you spread the word.

Now we'll explain the pre-printed postcards. After you speak with the neighbors, ask them to take a stack of the postcards (at least 10 per person), and address them to friends and neighbors in the district. When I had these cards printed and was part of a team running, the front side of the card had a picture of the candidates and their names and "Vote in the Democratic Primary September 12 –

for Responsive Democratic Government" in bold type. On the backside of the postcard, on the left was a place to personalize the intended recipient and a space below the message to allow an additional message and a place for the signature. For example:

Dear
I have met and talked with (first names). They are dedicated, responsive people and their spirit of public service have impressed me tremendously. Their honesty and vigor are what we need in politics today, and I ask you to join me in voting for them in the Democratic Primary on September 12th.
Sincerely,

The right side of the card back had space for the address and stamp. The union bug and authority line are printed small and vertical between them as a divider.

While we asked people in attendance to take at least ten, we encouraged people to address cards to their Christmas card list, family, people they were in clubs with, virtually everyone they knew who lived in the district.

You will have folks who will offer to take a stack of postcards and will promise to mail them out. Don't agree to it. Even those with the best of intentions may not get around to addressing and mailing the postcards. Instead, insist that they address the postcards and return them to Ashley, (the host), and your office will pick them up and pay for the postage. Having the host collect the postcards will provide you a much greater return. This is guaranteed the best way to achieve the desired outcome. It's also important that Ashley know that collecting the postcards is one of her duties related to hosting the tea. The purpose of these events is to speak to those in the room and to hopefully have them work for you by bringing more people into your camp.

One of our best strategies was to collect and hold on to the postcards and decide the optimum time for dropping them in the mail. We had volunteers put stamps on them and dropped them in the mail when we needed to create a buzz. For example, when we held onto the cards until 2-3 weeks before Election Day, we heard from voters that they received cards from their barber, neighbor, cousin, etc. For anyone that was still on the fence about who to vote for, this worked well as an endorsement for me.

I attended coffees and teas, (sometimes beer and wine were served), with just a handful of people present. There were other times when so many people attended it was hosted in the backyard. I had to stand on a chair to be seen and heard. I worked to maintain the same level of enthusiasm no matter how large or small the crowd. *Keep in mind that when you work these events well, you are not just talking to the people in the room or backyard, but all the possible voters in your district that those present know.*

Elections can be lost by a handful of votes. Just as candidates must understand the importance of the door-to-door canvass so must you understand the importance of evening functions such as coffees and teas. The only reason not to have one following a day of canvassing is if there is a larger function held in its place such as a community meeting, debate, bull roast or another fundraiser.

How valuable are coffees and teas to your campaign? A new highway threatened part of my district. As mentioned earlier, my team and I were known as the "stop the highway activists who were running for office." In one threatened precinct we held 12 teas in 12 blocks. And we won that particular precinct 8 to 1 over the opposition! Driving through the neighborhood the number of cars with our bumper stickers, and lawns with our yard signs were overwhelming. We were on the right side of an issue that was indeed very personal to many people. They invited us into their living rooms and supported us at the polls.

After the evening event, it's time to stop by the office, take care of any loose ends from the day or paperwork still waiting to be done. Strategizing with other candidates on the team may be necessary. Some candidates will be campaigning full time, and others will be working full time and be campaigning part-time. So if you are part of a ticket, you'll need to make time to meet with the other candidates when everyone's schedule allows. Then it's time to go home to sleep, wake up, and begin the schedule all over again.

17 MULTI-DWELLING RESIDENCES AND COMMUNITY GROUPS

The walk list is essential for identifying where your voters live in the district. Also, as you peruse the list, you will notice addresses where there may be a concentration of voters. These addresses can be college dorms, assisted living facilities or nursing homes, etc.. Gaining access to such facilities can be a challenge. However, the payoff for reaching a group of possible voters in one location is worth the challenge.

Multi-Dwelling Residences

Perhaps, there is an assisted living facility in your district. To start, ask if a volunteer on your staff knows anyone living or working in the facility. If someone working for you has a parent or grandparent at a particular assisted living, then chances are management will be more cooperative with allowing a candidate access. On the other hand, if the group dwelling you are trying to enter has "No Soliciting" signs posted then ask to see a manager. In a manner as non-confrontational as possible, you must tell the manager that you are not soliciting but exercising your constitutional right of free speech to speak to the voters in your district. If in fact, you are prevented access and "invited" to leave literature behind be sure to address it to the voters in the facility that are registered to your party. If campaign literature has someone's name on it, it is more likely to be received than if you merely hand a stack of literature to a front desk employee.

When I ran for office, there were also situations when I called the management of a senior living center or nursing home in advance and asked if they would assemble the residents to attend a group meeting. This saved me from stopping by every door providing there was a decent turnout. By calling ahead, I also had the fortune to be invited to speak in the dining room when residents were eating lunch or dinner.

There was also a very large assisted living facility in my district that would not allow us to meet with the residents or leave literature to be distributed. However, one of the residents was formerly involved in past campaigns and wanted to continue to help. He asked for several hundred pieces of campaign literature, and he worked the assisted living for us! And since other candidates were prevented access as were we, this worked to our advantage.

I addressed campaign literature to an Episcopal Convent in my district and successfully earned their votes. On another occasion, I canvassed a Roman Catholic Missionary Order that had taken a vow of silence. Greeted at the door by a young apostolate, she led me without speaking to Mother Superior who was allowed to speak. After our meeting, she accepted my campaign literature and assured me she would distribute it among the Sisters. On Election Day I stood at their polling station to watch the nuns' station wagon make repeated trips to drop off and pick up nuns as they voted. Many of them smiled and nodded at me as they walked up to the polling place.

Community Groups and Organizations

Senior Citizens, in particular, have the largest turnout among voters. Often they are the easiest demographic for a candidate to reach. Seniors are home more, some assemble in senior centers, and many are interested in local government and issues relative to their community.

There were senior centers that invited me to lunch regularly, and I was permitted to speak to some groups monthly. There were at least five senior centers in my district. I nurtured a relationship with these folks. I listened to their concerns, I ate with them, and I worked to gain their trust. After I won my first election, I continued the relationship and enjoyed stopping in once a month and having lunch with them. I knew many of these seniors by name. They were great supporters and also helped their friends who had physical difficulties get to the polls.

Veteran groups can be a challenge depending on the demographics of the district. In fact, if the politics of the group is heavily divided you may not be invited to speak as a candidate. However, don't dismiss other ways by which to access the group. Do you have a friend, associate, or relative in a veterans group? Ask to attend a meeting or an event as a guest. You may not have the opportunity to speak, but as you work the room, you will be introduced by the person who invited you, to veterans in the group. And it's also possible that you will be introduced or "singled out" and your presence announced to the group. In both of these examples, you are provided exposure to the group and showing your support for the veterans too.

PTA's work diligently *not* to be political. However, if you work hard on an issue that affects the community as I did with the "Stop the Highway" Committee, you have a platform to speak to the PTA before you are a candidate. If you have no reason to speak to the PTA on an issue, it's still imperative to be an active member of your children's PTA. Word will get around that you're running for office. This fact alone can win you votes. The same scenario applies to campaigning within the Recreation and Parks Council.

Neighborhood pools host dinners for adults to get together. I was invited by a supporter to join him and his wife and eat at their table. While far from an official event, he introduced me to his friends that belonged to the pool as a candidate running for The House of Delegates. The subtlety of the "silent endorsement" by the friend who casually introduced me to his neighbors was a powerful way to get in front of voters. In the same manner, find ways to be invited as a guest to PTA's, neighborhood homeowner associations and other neighborhood events. While it's not appropriate as a candidate, it is as a resident or an invited friend of someone in attendance. Your presence will resonate with voters.

Churches and the groups within them are also organizations comprised of voters you will want to reach. Some churches have an anathema to having anything at all to do with politics and others who are very political and sermonize to their congregants how they should vote. I found that many churches with primarily African American congregants had ministers who worked diligently to turn out their congregation to vote. In particular, where there are states with early voting on Sunday, the minister or pastor will hold a pep rally of sorts after a service and the congregation will then caravan to polling places. I was once invited to speak directly to a congregation from the pulpit. Also, many churches have Ladies Auxiliaries and other organizations that offer opportunities to reach voters.

Political clubs are a wonderful source for volunteers to work on your campaign. Many have experience and are skilled and embrace involvement in politics.

There still is value to attending meetings in a political club where incumbents are popular. There are always opportunities where some people in the room don't like the incumbent and are looking for a better candidate. These are the folks that often will become part of your army. Also, if you beat the incumbent, you're not alien to the club and will find that many people will transition to you as their favorite candidate.

If you know far in advance that you will be running against an established organization of incumbents, consider starting a club of your own. Although this is best done years in advance of the election, it remains beneficial to have a presence at the established club. It is a great way to build a group of supporters with people who share your political ideas and values. When I started a political club years before I decided to run, the people I met became my greatest supporters and worked in my campaigns.

In summary, identify opportunities to campaign in multi-residences such as dorms, assisted livings, etc. It's also important to seek as many community groups and organizations as possible for campaigning. While working to access multi-residences and organizations make for a bit more work, it is well worth it in the end if you have acquired the support from a wider base of people.

18 UTILIZING THE MEDIA AND GOOD PR

The effective use of media is dependent on the circumstances where you are running for office. When considering media, there is traditional media: newspapers, radio and TV. It's also necessary to create a relevance today using social media. In fact, it's vital to reach young voters under the age of 35.

Roles of Traditional Media

In some towns, there's a dominant newspaper that connects and is read by the community. In fact, the smaller the community, the more important traditional media is in reaching voters. However, as newspapers struggle across the country, this is becoming increasingly rare. Metropolitan newspapers are often prohibitively expensive, and many smaller community newspapers have ceased publishing.

If you live in a town where there is no relevant newspaper, you will need to rely on a direct mail campaign, (brochures, postcards and letters), to reach voters.

As a candidate representing a suburb of the city of Baltimore, radio and TV were too expensive to consider. There were three major TV stations for instance, and the cost of effectively producing and running commercials was prohibitive. Also, the size of the market for the radio and TV spots far exceeded my district. I would be paying to reach an audience of voters who could not vote for me. On the other hand, I served with fellow legislators from the Eastern Shore and rural Western Maryland where there was a single dominant radio and local TV station. Running commercials on radio and TV in that market was affordable in connecting with voters.

With the diversification of cable stations, there is also a possibility that you can buy a specific package of stations that are zoned. Once again, do your homework and be sure that the geographic zone covers the area where your voters live, and the demographic target of the cable station package is likely to be viewed by the voters you want to reach.

It's also important to be smart about how you spend your money when buying ad space in newspapers, local magazines or airtime. For example, I watched some candidates spend frivolously on full-page ads week after week and lose the election. I bought ads on occasion but did not spend money on full-page ads.

However, I worked very hard before I was a candidate writing editorials on behalf of the "Stop the Highway" committee. There were regular press releases on the issue as well. I was mentioned in the press releases, and as a result, I was often interviewed for articles. My name was regularly in front of the voters related to issues important to the community. It was great press, more powerful than a paid ad and it didn't cost any money. I wrote newspaper articles on community issues before running for office and once elected was offered the opportunity to write a weekly column. Writing a weekly column was an invaluable opportunity to remain in front of my constituency.

At the local level, there is an opportunity to befriend reporters and editors of newspapers and TV and radio stations. As a community leader, make a point to introduce yourself to key media players. In every market, there is local programming with writers and on-air personalities who welcome a "go to" person on matters involving the communities. When a story is written about certain issues in your community, you will likely be phoned for a comment or quote—a great way to get your name out among the voters. Once you've declared your candidacy, however, reputable media outlets may ask you for a point of view on a community issue, but they will also ask your opponent in the interest of fairness. A final advantage to creating alliances in the media is that if you become a subject of an article, the writer may be friendlier than not.

Pitfalls of Traditional Media

"Any press is good press as long as they spell your name correctly."
I have found this to be a false statement.

When an opponent uses the media to attack you, it's important to learn when to defend yourself and when to walk away. It's difficult not to defend yourself when an opponent is targeting you, but it's more important to keep it positive and work to change the focus on the issues. That said I found at times needing to defend myself against the attacks so the attack would not become a defining moment for me or my campaign. I also found that after volleying back and forth, voters appeared grateful when I returned to the issues. The challenge is knowing when to walk away and take the high road.

Reporters are sometimes given specific stories to write.

There are reputable journalists who investigate write and fact check their articles. They are accountable for what they write and handle the power they bestow in reporting news and politics responsibly. However, there is also a growing number of "writers" many who freelance or blog and write a piece in the hope of selling it. Additionally, some reporters are instructed to write with a particular idea or point of view in mind and gather the "facts" to support it. Both are versions of "tails wagging the dog." As a candidate running for office, be wary of both scenarios.

I was once grilled for half an hour by a reporter who was given the mandate to write a negative article about my former opponent. The reporter was looking for a quote from me. I talked to them at length in an attempt not to anger the reporter but also worked hard not to say any three words that could be taken out of context. The reporter needed a quote to substantiate the article. There were many times in the conversation when the reporter would repeatedly say to me such things as: "Is it not true that......" or "would you then say....." Ultimately, such a misstep could force you into a bad position on an issue or with your colleagues. Caught in the crosshairs, you may find you are the subject or at least a player in a piece meant to be sensational.

Beware of the Misquote

I learned that any five words published out of context or words omitted altogether could change the meaning of an otherwise factual statement. I once had an in-depth conversation with a reporter for a local paper on the three strategies I used when voting on bills before me in the Legislature.

First, I explained that I considered it my duty as a representative to vote the wishes of my constituents and not arrogantly vote what I think is right despite what they think.

Secondly, I explained that sometimes you voted for something that didn't affect your constituents. In such cases, I voted in such a way to support a fellow legislator in another district who had an interest in passing a certain bill that indeed did affect his constituents. This "trading" of sorts was done to rally support I may need down the road for a bill that would affect my constituents.

Finally, there were occasions when I had to vote my conscience against my constituents' wishes for moral reasons and then would have to work to change their minds or suffer the consequences.

After this conversation, an editorial in *The Baltimore Sun* took a position against how the county delegation voted on the governance of the community college. While quoting various senators, the reporter stated: Senator Hickman said, "I don't vote what I think is right despite what they think." While arguably my words, taken out of context and with the omission of other words it was far from the truth.

On another occasion, I was "trapped" by a reporter and a fellow politician. While I was in the legislature, I supported reform of not allowing campaigns to pay campaign workers on Election Day in Baltimore City to "walk around" handing out brochures and sample ballots. For example, in the past, a city councilman or senator could go to a higher office candidate and ask for "walk around" money to pay their "volunteers" on Election Day. Historically, the candidate who provided the most money could count on that city councilman or senator for support when running for a higher office. I believed this was a major source of corruption in the election process and came dangerously close to "buying an election." I pushed very strongly in committee to end it. The bill had gone to the floor for a vote.

Shortly after that, a city politician was talking to me casually in a bar and asked me if I believed everyone that used "walk around money" was corrupt. In an effort not to be confrontational and not accuse him of any wrongdoing and also knowing that you never know whose vote you might need one day, I soft-pedaled. What I didn't know was that the man sitting next to him was a reporter and the city politician was attempting to prove that I was insincere in my convictions.

In summary, use the media to your best advantage. Become the go-to person on major community issues. Be thoughtful when voicing concerns and opinions. Be concise, be careful and always pay attention to who may be listening.

Roles of a Website and Social Media

It's imperative to have a website to be relevant in today's political landscape. It's fundamentally important both for reaching and engaging young and older voters alike. It also offers a candidate the opportunity to post their platform including of course any "hot" issues of interest to their community. Use it as a place to have your bio and what makes you a qualified and earnest candidate. In essence, treat the website as a "live brochure." In addition to your qualifications and hot issues, include video of you in the community. Think about testimonials either written or videotaped of people telling why they intend to vote for you.

A website is used to have voters ask questions, sign up as volunteers and make contributions.

It also provides a place to discuss as the campaign "heats up," any misinformation that your opponent or the media may have circulated either through social media or traditional media. And be sure to use the website address in all campaign literature in addition to listing any of the social media platforms where you maintain a presence.

Facebook is also an effective tool for connecting with voters. Create a professional Facebook page for your campaign. Here the tone needs to be conversational yet professional. Start by gathering as many names as possible to "friend" or "like" you. Start with everyone you know in your universe: family, friends, colleagues, neighbors and supporters. Ask your supporters and volunteers to like your page. Use it wisely as a place to gather, excite and grow your base. Your Facebook page is an opportunity to reach voters on a daily basis. Ask your campaign staff and volunteers to post pictures and write posts about what you are doing every day.

Think about how knocking on doors can be made more effective when the voter allows their picture to be taken with the candidate or near a yard sign. It's likely that the voter will spread the Facebook photo and post and as a result, you have the opportunity to reach additional voters. In the same manner, when volunteers or supporters show up in your Facebook posts with a sign or a video as to why they are supporting you, and they share among their friends, co-workers, neighbors, etc., you have the opportunity to reach more voters.

As the candidate, it's important that you don't merely preach here and say what your vision is for the community. Address specific problems and your solutions if elected. Provide your vision for improving the community you want to represent. In addition to regular posts, provide links (such as an article you wrote), and a video of you campaigning or giving a speech or meeting voters. Provide solutions to problems in the here and now as well. Perhaps it's as simple as contact information you provided a voter in dealing with a problem in the community. Encourage questions or comments using Facebook, and above all ask your followers to like and share so your posts gain more visibility.

In addition to creating a Facebook page and creating posts, you can also use Facebook to reach other voters in your district by boosting your post. Boosting is a paid Facebook function where your posts are sent to all of your followers and an additional target audience for a minimal investment.

There are also social media companies that can assist in creating ads that pop up alongside Facebook when someone in your district is on their Facebook page. While Facebook ads are more expensive than boosting, it provides an opportunity to reach more voters and refine the desired demographic more than boosting a post through Facebook.

The same social media companies that create and run Facebook ads that pop up alongside a user's Facebook page also sell targeted online ads such as website banners and YouTube videos. In the same manner, as with Facebook ads, you can target all the voters in your district with this type of social media marketing.

While Twitter is another form of social media used in statewide and national elections, it may have little relevance for a local election. Consider the demographics of your voters such as age and median income, (not everyone has a smartphone), the size of the district you are running in, etc. It may not be worth the effort to build a Twitter following. On the other hand, if you surmise it may help to increase the conversation especially among young voters in your district, by all means, have a Twitter presence. You can link your Twitter and Facebook posts so that everything you post on Facebook goes out on Twitter.

Instagram is another social media outlet much like Twitter in that it may have limited value in a local campaign. However, with all the pictures needed for the Facebook posts, there is no extra work required to have them posted on Instagram and shared on Facebook.

Snapchat is more important at the moment in bigger races than local campaigns. It's worth noting that social media is changing at a fast pace. There certainly will be additional forms of social media to explore in the future and what works in a campaign today may not work two years from now.

Your website and social media presence as with many other campaign functions as mentioned earlier in the book is best left up to your staff and volunteers. As a candidate, you need to concentrate on meeting the voters and securing their support.

Finally, with consideration of everything discussed here regarding social media if the size of your campaign and budget allows, there is campaign management software such as NGP/Van that develops websites, accepts contributions online, offers email engagement, and social media organizational tools.

Pitfalls of a Website and Social Media

The only pitfall of using a website and social media is making the mistake that it's enough. These are additional tools for communicating with voters. They should be used to the maximum potential and will complement traditional media, as well as your efforts as a viable candidate working to connect with voters, face to face in your community.

19 ENDORSEMENTS

Caution: Tread Carefully

There are many arguments on the value of the endorsement. Every candidate wants to be endorsed. The question is: how many votes can an endorsement bring you? The answer is: it depends on the power of the endorsement. Add to that the fact that not all endorsements are created equal.

In fact, you don't find groups to endorse you; they will find you. You will need someone who can work with you to fill out endorsement interview questionnaires from organizations. It can be someone on your Campaign Committee that you trust explicitly, or perhaps a strategist who can help you navigate through endorsement questionnaires. What seems "easy" is not only time consuming but fraught with risks.

First off, it's important to decide if the hours invested in the paperwork and perhaps interviews are worth the endorsement. Does the organization have a possible ten people in your district or hundreds?

Secondly, be careful which endorsement questionnaires you fill out. There are bound to be groups that you may choose not to be affiliated with at all. And be aware that certain groups will do nothing to support you and win over voters, but are merely looking to get you on the record and when you're elected hold your feet to the fire when voting on an issue they asked you about on a questionnaire.

As a candidate use caution as you seek endorsements. There is a natural inclination to want to say the right thing to please or appease a group. As stated earlier, be true to your stand on the issues. Don't pander to groups to seek their support. Endorsement questionnaires also serve as a public written record of your viewpoints. And you can be sure if there is cause to change how you vote on an issue once in office it will become known that you waffled.

77

WaPo, WT, Ward Examiner?

Endorsements Worth Seeking

One of the most important endorsements for a candidate is from your local newspaper. While newspapers are undoubtedly struggling for their viability in today's world of digital media, overall they still provide an opportunity to reach and possibly influence thousands of voters. Most newspapers offer digital subscriptions aimed at younger audiences or anyone who relies on reading the news on a computer or mobile device. And don't overlook community newspapers in your district. Again, it's the opportunity to be endorsed or given the stamp of approval by a respected voice in the community and reach a large audience.

There are usually no questionnaires by newspapers because it is unnecessary. Reporters are often seeking candidates' stands on issues for stories they are writing. The best advice is to make yourself available for comment, communicate well, be accessible and by that, I mean to be sensitive to the deadlines of journalists. If they call with a question, for example, you want to seize the opportunity to provide a reply as they are undoubtedly calling your opponent as well.

If there is a viable community newspaper in your district, visit and get to know the editor. They will be much more approachable.

In addition to a newspaper's endorsements which trickle onto the editorial pages of the paper starting a few weeks before the election, newspapers will print a summary on Election Day of their endorsements. *The Baltimore Sun* was the prominent paper in the district where I ran. On Election Day I witnessed as voters came to the polls with the tearsheet from the newspaper in hand with their list of endorsements.

The first time I ran for office I was a green enthusiastic idealist and 24 years old. Knowing an endorsement from the most powerful media voice in the district would propel my campaign I called the City Desk of *The Sun* and was transferred to a secretary who passed me to another secretary who put my call through. I said that I was a young person running for office for the first time and I wanted to know how to obtain an endorsement from *The Sunpapers*. I was invited down to a meeting.

I was excited and thought I was going to be interviewed by someone in the newsroom. I checked in through security and was directed to the newsroom. Next, I was led through the newsroom to a hallway. I entered a tastefully decorated paneled office away from the noisy din of the newsroom, where two secretaries sat behind desks. They asked who I was to meet with and then took me through to another paneled office where a private secretary sat behind a large desk. She announced my arrival and I walked into the office of the Editor-in-Chief. He sat down and talked with me for an hour.

On the way out of *The Baltimore Sun,* I ran into someone I knew, the Chief Campaign Aide for an incumbent Congressman running for re-election. He asked what I was doing there. When I told him, he shook his head in disbelief and said the Congressman had been trying to set up an appointment with him for over three weeks and couldn't get a returned phone call.

The Editor-in-Chief directed the editor to send out a journalist, and she wrote a feature article on the editorial page about how I, as a young person was going about my first run for office. The article included the nuts and bolts of the office, the volunteers and how we were campaigning. In the end, I also received their endorsement. Sometimes you need to take chances. I would not have been featured in an article or received an endorsement if I hadn't taken a risk.

While newspapers are an important endorsement, there are certainly others that are also important. Unions, for example, send out questionnaires to decide who they will back in an election. Questionnaires can prove to be very helpful as an opportunity to state your positions publicly on issues and be endorsed by organizations. When I ran for office, not only were there multiple endorsement questionnaires to be completed, but I was asked to attend an AFL-CIO meeting with the heads of various unions in attendance for an interview. Gratefully my stand on the issues was in line with their objectives, and I did receive backing.

At this meeting not only did they ask questions about my stand on issues, but they examined my campaign literature to be sure it was marked with the union bug which is a small icon that identifies all printed matter as produced in a union shop. If you're a Democrat or seeking support from a union, it's an often unforgivable mistake to have materials printed in a non-union shop. In addition to campaign literature our stationery, buttons, and bumper stickers were printed at businesses where employees had a union, and we always asked to have the union bug printed on the item.

A union endorsement is beneficial in many different ways. First, they send out mailings to their members endorsing you as a candidate. Depending on the profile of the demographic in your district that can translate to a great many votes!

When I was running for re-election, the labor unions were again supportive this time partially because of my stand on certain issues that affected their members. The local building trade construction union assembled, erected and maintained our signs. The unions also supported us through their purchase of tickets and presence at our fundraisers.

Another powerful union is The County Teachers Association. There are times at least in my State where they endorse candidates from both parties. For instance, in the district, there may be 5 or 6 candidates running for the lower house. The County Teachers Association will choose three candidates and they may choose two Democrats and one Republican.

The Teachers Association had particularly challenging questionnaires and endorsement interviews. Once endorsed the support extended beyond its' membership. For instance, schools close Election Day, so there was usually a teacher or two on hand to work each poll. They would greet voters, who often were the parents of their students and hand out a card with an apple graphic on it that listed the candidates who supported public education.

I also had the good fortune of knowing a man who lived in my district who was a paid staff member in the County Teachers Association. He was instrumental in turning out teachers now and then as volunteers in our campaign headquarters.

While on the subject of unions and associations another organization to pay attention to are churches. Although most do not officially endorse candidates citing the separation of Church and State, there are times when a group of ministers will publish the Ministerial Alliance endorsement and identify candidates they think are in line with their teachings.

In summary, endorsements are valuable as a method of reaching members of groups with a recommendation to vote for you. They can also help through volunteering for the campaign and fundraising. Be sure the group aligns with your stand on the issues and be certain that the time invested answering questionnaires and follow-up interviews are worth the amount of influence they yield.

20 RALLIES, PARADES AND COMMUNITY EVENTS

R allies are hosted by the candidate to inspire and excite the base. They are also a conduit to connect with voters who are on the fence about who will earn their vote. Rallies can also bring media attention which in turn brings light to a candidate and local issues.

Whenever there is an opportunity to meet voters at a community event, festival or parade it's important to do it. There will be rules as to which events welcome candidates and rules governing candidates' participation. Be sure to have someone in your campaign headquarters research upcoming events and the criteria to participate long before the event.

While I hosted rallies and family fun events, I also attended every festival and community event possible. Rules varied as to the extent we could represent ourselves and the office we were seeking, but we either worked the event openly or with subtlety.

Fourth of July, in particular, was celebrated with great fanfare in our district, and we made a whole day of the festivities. There were no speeches, no discussion of community issues, but a wonderful opportunity to build name recognition and provide a face with the name.

To maximize the opportunity and be in the parade, we asked a volunteer with ties to a car dealership to allow us to borrow a convertible. On other occasions, we asked owners and supporters to drive us in their convertible or antique car. Be sure the car is an American brand. We were able to sit on the top of the backseat, and in addition to waving to crowds along the parade route, we (when allowed) threw candy to the children. At times this was not allowed as a concern for children endangered by moving vehicles and adults walking the parade route. What I found more effective than candy was to have volunteers handing out helium balloons to children along the parade route with our names on them.

Two communities in my district had different rules for allowing candidates to participate in their parades. We adapted to the rules, so we were able to ride in both parades. For instance, we were allowed signage in one parade with our names and offices we were running for, but in the second community parade, candidates were allowed signage with their name but not the office. Incumbents, however, were allowed signage with name and office. We complied by having signs created that were in two pieces with the office "covered" up by another piece of cardboard attached by string for the second parade.

During the parade, I left the car for part or the entire parade route while my spouse and other candidates rode in the car. Volunteers walked with me wearing straw hats with bumper stickers on them; they wore T-shirts and wore many campaign buttons. Walking provided the opportunity to shake hands, introduce myself, make eye contact, point and wave to people I knew in the crowd and smile, smile, smile. It was heartening to walk the crowds and be cheered by a supporter leading the crowd in cheers, and it was tough to continue smiling as the parade wrapped through an area penetrated by my opponents.

A volunteer's teenage daughter who had learned to stilt walk wore a sandwich board with the names of the candidates. With her father at her side, she walked the parade route and contributed to the fun atmosphere and undoubtedly added attention.

After the parade, there were additional opportunities at the Soapbox Derby and then a community picnic and fireworks. It was a full day of festivities, meeting and greeting supporters and voters in the district. It was not a day for issues or politics in the traditional campaign context, yet it was an invaluable day for meeting voters and building a presence in the communities. And be prepared – if done well, your face will hurt from smiling at the end of the day.

21 CANDIDATE FORUMS & DEBATES

Candidate forums are a great opportunity to be seen and heard by groups of people to win over voters.

A forum can be a debate between candidates or an opportunity for multiple candidates, one at a time, to offer a presentation of their candidacy and issues that are sometimes followed by questions from the audience. Groups or organizations that host forums can include senior centers, political clubs, colleges, cable television stations in mid-size markets, a local television station in single markets, business associations, minority organizations and special interest groups such as environmental organizations, or professional associations.

As a candidate, an opportunity to make a presentation and answer questions or debate your opponent may result in an official endorsement from the club or organization. While that may help you win voters, even in situations where there is no endorsement it remains a worthwhile opportunity to win over voters a group at a time.

Attending a political club, for instance, is helpful for reaching a group of likely voters and informs members of your stand on local issues. It provides the opportunity to build your volunteer army *and* possibly earn the club's endorsement.

One particular organization that has remained a powerful and respected political voice over the years is The League of Women Voters.

The League of Woman Voters is a non-partisan organization dedicated to empowering and educating voters in over 700 State and local leagues. The organization hosts debates and candidate forums and in many areas publishes their well - known Voters Guides.

The Voters Guides are available online. Sometimes they are distributed as a supplement to a newspaper, mailed to homes or available free in public places such as libraries. Often it is distributed as a combination of the above.

The guide provides candidates a fixed number of words for biographical information. All candidates running for a particular office are asked a series of questions to answer in a fixed number of words, and the questions and responses are published in The Voters' Guide.

The demographics of the readers of the Voters Guide are one of an intelligent voter who is making an effort to understand the positions of candidates.

As a candidate, I encourage you to spend the time and effort to respond to their questionnaires thoughtfully. Providing well thought out positions on the questions asked can earn you votes. Not responding or missing the deadline to respond to the questions they send will result in your name and a "no response" listing. Not answering thoughtfully, can be embarrassing and will lose you votes.

Forums or debates are an opportunity to connect with groups of voters which is always an advantage as you work in your district to secure more votes.

22 SURVEYS

S urveys can provide a wealth of information before and during your campaign. As a candidate, if you desire to have surveys conducted it's imperative to have them conducted scientifically under the supervision of a professional. Surveys are only as good as the information they provide, and even then they are at times off base.

Professionally conducted surveys are expensive and not suitable for many local elections. I had the good fortune to have as a supporter a Professor of Sociology at the local university. He organized the survey, developed the questions and trained the survey takers.

Carefully evaluate the value of surveys for your campaign beyond the expense. There are advantages and clear disadvantages to implementing surveys.

A clear advantage to surveying your voters is to check on "hot button" issues. As a candidate, it's very easy to assume that a certain issue is of primary concern to your voters to learn that it's another issue that takes precedence. Taken a step further, perhaps one area of your district puts a certain issue ahead of another. Such information is valuable as you conduct the door-to-door canvass in all the communities in your district.

Secondly, it can be helpful to know how you're doing in the campaign in relation to who will vote for you. Perhaps the survey has you with a comfortable lead against your opponent. You can sigh in relief and coast to the finish line. On the other hand, the survey can reveal you are trailing your opponent by a small margin. As the candidate, it gives you the opportunity to make some changes and do whatever is possible to close the gap.

Now let's consider the disadvantages. To start, sometimes for whatever reason surveys are dead wrong. Next, you have the situation as mentioned previously where the survey reveals you are comfortably ahead. Do you coast as you wait for the clock to run out? Do your supporters work less thinking the election is "in the bag"? And if you and your supporters become comfortable and a bit lazy will that affect the election? On the flip side, what if the survey reveals your opponent has the lead by double digits? Do you keep campaigning? Do your supporters give up? In short, the results of a survey can de-motivate you.

In conclusion, as a candidate, you must weigh the advantages and disadvantages of using surveys during your campaign. You must consider the value of the information vs. the resources it would consume. In the end, it may prove to be more beneficial to devote both money and volunteers needed for surveys to actively campaigning.

23 ELECTION DAY

When you're a candidate running for office, Election Day is undoubtedly one of the longest days of your life. If you campaigned well you are exhausted, nervous, excited and although the finish line is clearly in sight, there is still more to do to make sure every possible vote you have worked for is cast and counted and that your volunteers know what needs to be done on the final day.

Like every move you make during the campaign, the key is advance planning. To start, you may need a town hall or some rentable room where all your volunteers can meet election night after the polls close. Working on the logistics for the election night party needs to be done many weeks before the election. If your headquarters is large enough, you can stage the after party there. The obvious advantage is the cost savings. The money saved by not renting a room can be utilized elsewhere.

As the candidate, it is important to realize that you have brought many people with you for this ride, and they will want to share in the results. Hopefully, the gathering will be a victory party, but if it isn't they will still need to be together, share "war" stories and you'll need to have them together to thank them for their dedication and hard work.

Another necessary task after schools close on Monday and before polls open on Tuesday, Election Day (if local Election Laws allow), is the collection of yard signs to be used at polling places. Volunteers will need to go through neighborhoods and remove yard signs and place them around polling places. You want as many signs as feasible to greet the voters on Election Day. If your opponent has six signs and you have twelve, it appears as though you are the favored candidate.

Poll Coverage

Someone on your staff needs to research previous elections to uncover the typical turnout by precinct for the primary or general election (whichever it is) and estimate the number of sample ballots needed by each precinct. If it's a new precinct or a precinct that has been split, then an educated guess will do.

In addition to consideration of the number of voters served at a polling place, you must consider the pattern of voters approaching the entrance. Are they entering the building from two different places or is the entrance to the polling place such that the main entrance is located halfway on a semi-circle driveway with people walking up from two different directions? Walking patterns and where cars are parked will determine the minimal number of volunteers needed to cover that polling place.

If you have early voting, it's important to schedule Poll Workers to cover early voting locations as long as it is permitted to do so by your Election Authority.

Once that is completed, volunteers can work assembling bags labeled by precinct which will include sample ballots, buttons, schedule of who is scheduled every hour, phone number of headquarters, and Circuit Riders. The bags will also include watcher slips which are signed permission slips from the candidate, if permitted by local Election Laws, enabling Poll Watchers (also called Watchers/Challengers), to go inside the polling places. Include a tally sheet for the Watcher to record the results once the polls close. Lastly, include a page of general instructions and anything else you may deem helpful for those working the polls.

Next, assign Precinct Captains who will be your eyes and ears at the polling places. They will manage volunteers at the polling places and interact as needed with the Poll Workers and Judges inside. It will be important to have a meeting with the Precinct Captains a few days before the election to give them their bags, instructions, and answer any questions. They will also need the schedule of volunteers for their precinct. Once the schedule is complete for each precinct, a master list provides the candidate and the Office Manager with a list of who is working at each precinct. The master list will help with troubleshooting to ensure thorough coverage at precincts as well as any last minute problems that may arise.

Be aware that scheduling volunteers at the polls will be a moving target. I found that some people will show up late and others will not show up at all. You will want to rely on the Precinct Captain to be responsible and call volunteers and do whatever is necessary to fill a spot outside the polling place. In the same manner, if the Precinct Captain is unsuccessful in filling the spot you want to depend on him or her calling headquarters and asking for help to have someone dispatched to the polling place as soon as possible.

I always had unpaid volunteers work the polls. However, there are communities and jurisdictions where it is tradition to pay Poll Workers. I caution you that it can lead to corruption. Here's how: say for example, as a candidate you need "walk around money" to pay your Poll Workers. Three candidates are running for Governor. One offers to provide you $5,000 to pay Poll Workers; the second candidate offers you $10,000 and the third candidate $15,000. You decide to go to the highest bidder. In return, you are expected to support that candidate regardless if your stand on the issues is in alignment with candidate #3. Take this a step further: it becomes very easy to pocket some of this money. In essence, you have sold out to the highest bidder. I believe that such conduct is unsavory and makes you unfit to work in government. It will, in fact, hurt you as a candidate at some point in your career.

That said there was a neighborhood in my district where the Poll Workers were very dedicated and had been working the polls for years. They insisted on money for gas and food on Election Day. Rather than pay them, we offered to reimburse the workers if they presented us with receipts. We offered the same to the other Poll Workers, and they declined. Your volunteers are people who support you because they share your vision of good government and improving their community. It all changes once money is involved.

My earliest memory of working the polls was when I was eight years old. My uncle was a Precinct Captain, and he had a short supply of literature. It was my job to run into the polling place and go through the trash can and find unfolded sample ballots, dust them off, stack them and bring them back out to my uncle to redistribute. We were early "recyclers." At the end of the day, he paid me $1. That was the first and only time I was paid to work the polls.

As you assign, Poll Workers and Precinct Captains pay attention to where you put people. For instance, a Precinct Captain or Poll Worker wearing your campaign T-shirt or a hat with your button on it who knows many people in the neighborhood can be very engaging with neighbors coming to vote. And who knows how many votes may swing your way because "Marc from down the street" is working to get you elected!

Some voters are annoyed at people trying to hand them a sample ballot so train your Poll Workers on etiquette. They should be engaging but not aggressive. Offer a sample ballot but don't try to force one upon voters. Instruct your workers as to the law regarding how close they can stand to the doors of the polling place. And instruct them if they see someone they know by all means greet them and mention how they are supporting you.

There are two main reasons to have Poll Workers on Election Day. First, if you don't have workers at the polls and your opponent does, then you don't look like a serious candidate. Secondly, outside the polling place is the last opportunity to swing a vote. Perhaps a worker engaged with a neighbor, or perhaps it was the result of a Poll Worker giving a sample ballot to someone who was still uncommitted.

Sample ballots are essential as a handout on Election Day. Additionally, they are more effective in your campaign (if your budget allows), mailed to voters before Election Day. If you are part of a ticket, the cost of mailing a sample ballot is shared by all candidates. A sample ballot is especially helpful for candidates who are running for offices further down the ballot. While many voters might show up to vote for a Mayor or State Senator, they may not have name recognition for names down ballot like the Central Committee.

Watch out for sample ballots being used for shenanigans on Election Day by unscrupulous politicians. There are sample ballots where a candidate will create a fake ticket aligning himself or herself with a front-runner. Fake sample ballots have been known to happen even across party lines in a general election.

On Election Day, as a candidate, your time is best spent at the polls. Having identified the busiest polls when working on the volunteer list, you'll know where you need to go. You may consider working outside the polling place where you grew up or where you live. If you identify yourself and the seat you are running for and hopefully put a sample ballot in some hands, you are likely to win more votes. As mentioned earlier, some voters know who they are voting for at the top of the ticket—Governor, and State Senator but when it comes to the lower house or the Central Committee they have not committed. Your interaction can make the difference.

Circuit Riders

Another important volunteer job is Circuit Rider. We divided the precinct into groups and each group had an assigned Circuit Rider. In my district of 125,000 people, we had four Circuit Riders. The job of the Circuit Rider is to drive between polling places and check on supplies. One poll may be low in campaign literature or sample ballots while another one has more than needed. Perhaps a Watcher Slip signed by the candidate is needed. A Circuit Rider confirms whether volunteers have shown up and troubleshoots if there is an issue with a Judge or a Poll Worker.

Circuit Riders can also ask volunteers to find out from Election Judges how many voters from your party's roll have been in to vote. The volunteer must remove all candidate and party affiliation from their clothes and then chat with judges. This information was valuable to me as a candidate to know how the turnout was and what we needed to do to get the vote out. If it was, 10 am in the morning for example and we had 800 on the poll book and 200 had already voted; we knew how many we needed to come out.

Circuit Riders also have the duty of making sure the troops are fed and hydrated. Weeks in advance of Election Day, our campaign secured plenty of food for our workers. We had 500 box lunches donated by a local union. I know of candidates who bought fast food lunches and others who had food donated by local restaurants or caterers who offered discounted food. We bought boxes of Dunkin Donuts Coffee and Circuit Riders traveled between polls distributing hot coffee, bagels and donuts. Once lunchtime rolled around, they passed out box lunches to our Poll Workers. Circuit Riders also carried soft drinks, energy bars and candy---everything possible to keep our volunteers satiated.

Poll Watchers/Challengers

The role of the Poll Watchers in states that allow candidates to appoint them is to act as a representative for the candidate. With a permission slip signed by the candidate, they are permitted to enter the polls to verify the process and make sure there are no mistakes willful or accidental. Not all Election Authorities allow candidates to choose Watchers. In some places, the party chooses.

In my early elections, we had voting machines with counter wheels inside them. A Watcher entered the polling place with the Election Judges before it was open to the public. It was their task to verify that all machines began at zero. If a machine had a count on it, a sign would be posted that the total votes for that particular machine for a certain candidate must be subtracted by the appropriate number at the end of the day. Likewise, in the case of electronic machines, tapes are run, and they must all reflect a zero before the first vote cast and a record made if they are not at zero.

We never had a problem with entering a polling place to verify the equipment. It's important the Watchers are respectful of the Judges and not interfere with them as they work. It's a long day, and while the Judges are trained, equipment and procedures change, and sometimes they become flustered. Poll Watchers must know that Circuit Riders are the first line of support or they can call the campaign headquarters for help in dealing with an unreasonable Election Judge.

While the polls are open, the Poll Watchers are allowed (in some jurisdictions), to enter the polling place and stand behind the Judges checking in voters. It is imperative that they do not disrupt the process or interrupt the Judges. As states and jurisdictions all over the country are switching to electronic poll books, this process will become more difficult.

There are places in the country where Challengers or Poll Watchers are permitted to challenge the identity of someone voting. Unfortunately, this tactic is used to intimidate voters and as a method to suppress votes. It's imperative to check with your Election Board or Election Authority as to the validity of the rules concerning Challengers.

There is something so inherently wrong with conduct meant to suppress votes. If your opponent participates in this behavior, your Poll Watcher/Challenger must contact your headquarters at once.

GOTV—Get Out The Vote

One crucial purpose of having the Poll Watcher inside the polling place if permitted by the Election Authority is to create a list of voter's who have voted. The list is passed to Poll Workers on the outside, which pass them to a Circuit Rider who takes them to headquarters. It is important to have a phone bank of volunteers ready to start calling the voters on the list who have not yet voted. And in the event the Election Laws are such that a Poll Watcher can't make a list of who has voted, or if it is too difficult to pull off, it remains important for volunteers to call voters in your district.

Today with cell phones, (no more hard wiring or hefty deposits necessary), it is much easier to assemble a team of volunteers to have them call voters who have not been to the polls. Starting with your 1's and then the 2's (refer to daily canvass, these are people you ranked most likely to vote for you), the callers will need a script of how to best encourage voters to get to the polls.

"Hi Mrs. Semone, This is Ryan at the Hickman-Murphy campaign office. Have you had a chance to vote today? Your vote is so important in this election. We hope you can make it to the poll. If you need a ride, we can arrange for one of our volunteers to pick you up and bring you to your polling place and take you back home."

If a babysitter was needed, we offered to babysit. If transportation was an issue, we offered to drive the voter. We worked at being as accommodating as possible while conveying the importance of their vote. If the voter said they intended to vote later in the afternoon, a volunteer followed up later with another call.

Calling voters is tedious work. We had a volunteer working the lists and helping to organize the process among callers. There was a person who reviewed the script and worked to keep the group enthusiastic. And we were sure to provide food and make the task as enjoyable as possible. While we preferred to have phone volunteers in the office to best check on progress and keep them motivated, we also had trusted stay at home moms and elderly volunteers who called from their homes.

There will be neighborhoods where you know through the results of your door-to-door canvass that you are favored to win. Assign volunteers to knock on doors and ask people if they have voted. Again, offer transportation, babysitting services whatever is needed to *Get Out The Vote*. Even good intentioned voters will find excuses not to vote. Impressing the importance of their vote and solving their "issue" preventing them from coming out to vote is imperative to winning an election. For instance, in a two-way primary, if 30% of the voters usually turn out to vote, the election is won with 16%. Working to win the additional 1% or 2% with GOTV activities is well worth assigning volunteers to knock on doors and call voters on the phone. In fact, it may make the difference in winning or losing.

In a recent election, I worked for a candidate running for the U.S. Senate. We had a late call in the evening from an elderly woman who was recently discharged from the hospital. She wanted to vote but had no way of getting to the polls. I went to her house, helped her to the car and drove her to the polling place. A kind Election Judge gave us a place to sit and moved her to the front of the line. She was frail, couldn't walk without assistance but was committed to the importance of her vote and the democratic process.

When the Polls Close

Once again it's crucial that the planning for this process is done long before Election Day beginning with finding out the rules in your state regarding Poll Watchers. In my State of Maryland, one or two Poll Watchers with required permission slips signed by the candidate are allowed inside the polls just before 8:00 pm as the last voters leave. As the candidate, I urge you to impress the importance to the Poll Watchers to be *inside* the building before the locking of the doors. Election Judges have had a long day, 13 + hours and there is still more to be done.

The Circuit Rider drives to every polling place in their district to confirm there are Poll Watchers ready to enter the polling places. It's also smart for Circuit Riders to have permission slips in their possession. If there is no Poll Watcher for a polling place, they will need to step up.

When mechanical voting machines were used, they had to roll out one at a time. A Democrat and Republican Election Judge read the numbers off poorly lit wheels from inside the machine as the head Election Judge sat before a big table with large sheets of paper and wrote down the numbers from the wheels. The candidates' Poll Watchers simultaneously recorded the numbers as they were read.

Electronic voting in most states, using either touch screens or scan screens of paper ballots has streamlined this process. When the polls close, each machine can automatically spit out a tape with the results and can print more than one copy. In my jurisdiction, the Election Judges taped them to a wall. As the election results of the precinct went up, the Poll Watchers would hover to peek at the number and write it down on the form they were given. Next, they would rush the results back to headquarters.

At your campaign headquarters, cover a large wall with paper or project on a large screen. As the Poll Watchers come back to headquarters, write the results for everyone to see. With calculators or smartphones in hand, your volunteers will add the precinct numbers a few times then post it on the wall. As a result, you may know "unofficially" if you have won or lost long before the Election Board/Election Authority runs the electronic modules, enters the results into a computer network which sends them to another jurisdiction where they will be published on a web page.

Victory Party

With hard work and sometimes a bit of luck you have won, and it's time to celebrate! If this is a primary win, you may soon be repeating the process all over again but on a larger scale. If this win is for the general election, you can finally take a deep breath knowing that the campaign is over although a good politician never stops campaigning altogether.

Your volunteers have assembled in the room you have rented. There is leftover food from today. There are snacks, beer, wine, soft drinks, cookies and cake. The TV is playing and even though you know the results the room erupts in cheers every time there is an announcement for the results of a precinct. Hugs and congratulations abound. And as excited as you are, as the candidate, you will realize how much this win also means to the many volunteers who worked long and hard for this night. When you make your acceptance speech, be sure you recognize that it is not your win but "our win."

The Losers Party

To no one's surprise, the gathering after a losing campaign is not much of a celebration. Most importantly, give a speech and thank all your volunteers for their time, and their dedication. No matter what you are feeling: disappointed, angry, frustrated, or exhausted, now is not the time to express it. Your volunteers need to know you value them. Don't be a bad loser. You may do this again in the future and will want their support. And even if you don't run again, it's vital that they leave feeling that they were a part of something good.

After Election Business

Assign volunteers to remove all large signs in the community. And be sure to have them check that signs are removed from polling places too.

It's time to shut down headquarters. Return borrowed equipment and furniture, and pay bills in preparation for closing up the office. There is some cleaning up to do. Next, there is preparation for assuming office and perhaps planning a party when you're sworn in.

Election Day Checklist

- Room rented for after party
- Have volunteers work on food donations or discounts for Election Day workers and after party
- Find out rules from local Election Board/Election Authority for Poll Watchers/ Challengers
- Research voting history at precincts
- Develop schedule for all workers needed on Election Day
- Have volunteers collect all necessary information and supplies and fill precinct bags
- Schedule a meeting and distribute bags to all Precinct Captains of supplies and review all duties
- Assign volunteers to pick up neighborhood signs and redistribute them at polling places the night before the election
- Develop and distribute script for telephone bank and volunteers working from home for GOTV
- Clean up crew for after party
- Make arrangements to take down large community signs and be sure polling stations have no more yard signs

24 YOU CAN MAKE A DIFFERENCE

I have been told more than once that for every honorable, person that does not run for office there is a scoundrel who will.

Running for the right reasons is rewarding and the greatest gift you can bestow on future generations. We share the responsibility to leave the world a better place beginning in our communities. And it takes honorable and idealistic visionaries to do it.

Plan, be smart and be efficient. Work hard. Every dollar spent in your campaign must earn a vote.

Meet your voters every day. Listen to their concerns and ask for their vote.

Conduct your campaign with honor and integrity. Win or lose you and your loyal supporters will look back with pride on the experience.

Run a positive campaign. Be sure that your message is always what you will do for your voters not why they should not vote for your opponent. If attacked by your opponent defend yourself but don't be pulled down into the mud. Maintain your honor and your voters will appreciate it.

If you decide to run, give it all you got. At the end of the campaign, there will be no regrets.

You can make a difference. Go for it!

Acknowledgements

Thanks to my running mates, supporters and volunteers who worked so diligently on our campaigns. Without your hard work and dedication to serving our communities, this book would never have been written. My life is richer as a result of the experiences we shared.

I also want to thank Tyler Carr, the Data Director for the Maryland Democratic Party, for helping me to understand how VoteBuilder/VAN Campaign Software can facilitate and propel a political campaign. While a technological advancement such as this will aid candidates in campaigning, I believe its real value is in giving candidates a greater opportunity to be in front of voters!

ABOUT THE AUTHORS

Timothy Hickman has had a passion for politics beginning as early as eight years old when he "worked" the polls with his uncle. His interest in politics advanced further as a young boy listening to the spirited political conversations around the family dinner table.

He was twenty-four years old the first time he ran for office. Timothy Hickman has served as a Delegate in the Maryland House of Delegates, and as a Senator in the Maryland State Senate. He has also served as a Member of the Baltimore County Democratic State Central Committee and as a Member of the Maryland Democratic Party State Executive Board. He served as an Alternate Member of the Baltimore County Board of Elections. Timothy Hickman teaches political science at the Community College of Baltimore County and is a campaign consultant.

Catherine Hickman has listened attentively to Tim's many interesting stories concerning the people, the commitment and the tough grind that went into a run for local office. On more than one occasion she mentioned that there was a book in the wealth of information he shared with her and a few others.

She has worked professionally in advertising and marketing for newspapers and a direct mail publication including a stint for The Washington Post where she traveled nationally for the paper and then later worked as The National Account Manager in New York and managed the New York office. She is a member of a Writers Group and the owner of CRH Marketing Solutions where she helps independently owned businesses market.

Timothy and Catherine reside in Baltimore County, Maryland and whenever possible escape to Marathon in the Florida Keys.

Made in the USA
Middletown, DE
23 December 2018